C-638   CAREER EXAMINATION SERIES

This is your
PASSBOOK for...

Purchasing Agent

Test Preparation Study Guide
Questions & Answers

COPYRIGHT NOTICE

This book is SOLELY intended for, is sold ONLY to, and its use is RESTRICTED to individual, bona fide applicants or candidates who qualify by virtue of having seriously filed applications for appropriate license, certificate, professional and/or promotional advancement, higher school matriculation, scholarship, or other legitimate requirements of education and/or governmental authorities.

This book is NOT intended for use, class instruction, tutoring, training, duplication, copying, reprinting, excerption, or adaptation, etc., by:

1) Other publishers
2) Proprietors and/or Instructors of "Coaching" and/or Preparatory Courses
3) Personnel and/or Training Divisions of commercial, industrial, and governmental organizations
4) Schools, colleges, or universities and/or their departments and staffs, including teachers and other personnel
5) Testing Agencies or Bureaus
6) Study groups which seek by the purchase of a single volume to copy and/or duplicate and/or adapt this material for use by the group as a whole without having purchased individual volumes for each of the members of the group
7) Et al.

Such persons would be in violation of appropriate Federal and State statutes.

PROVISION OF LICENSING AGREEMENTS – Recognized educational, commercial, industrial, and governmental institutions and organizations, and others legitimately engaged in educational pursuits, including training, testing, and measurement activities, may address request for a licensing agreement to the copyright owners, who will determine whether, and under what conditions, including fees and charges, the materials in this book may be used them. In other words, a licensing facility exists for the legitimate use of the material in this book on other than an individual basis. However, it is asseverated and affirmed here that the material in this book CANNOT be used without the receipt of the express permission of such a licensing agreement from the Publishers. Inquiries re licensing should be addressed to the company, attention rights and permissions department.

All rights reserved, including the right of reproduction in whole or in part, in any form or by any means, electronic or mechanical, including photocopying, recording, or by any information storage and retrieval system, without permission in writing from the Publisher.

Copyright © 2024 by
National Learning Corporation

212 Michael Drive, Syosset, NY 11791
(516) 921-8888 • www.passbooks.com
E-mail: info@passbooks.com

PUBLISHED IN THE UNITED STATES OF AMERICA

PASSBOOK® SERIES

THE *PASSBOOK® SERIES* has been created to prepare applicants and candidates for the ultimate academic battlefield – the examination room.

At some time in our lives, each and every one of us may be required to take an examination – for validation, matriculation, admission, qualification, registration, certification, or licensure.

Based on the assumption that every applicant or candidate has met the basic formal educational standards, has taken the required number of courses, and read the necessary texts, the *PASSBOOK® SERIES* furnishes the one special preparation which may assure passing with confidence, instead of failing with insecurity. Examination questions – together with answers – are furnished as the basic vehicle for study so that the mysteries of the examination and its compounding difficulties may be eliminated or diminished by a sure method.

This book is meant to help you pass your examination provided that you qualify and are serious in your objective.

The entire field is reviewed through the huge store of content information which is succinctly presented through a provocative and challenging approach – the question-and-answer method.

A climate of success is established by furnishing the correct answers at the end of each test.

You soon learn to recognize types of questions, forms of questions, and patterns of questioning. You may even begin to anticipate expected outcomes.

You perceive that many questions are repeated or adapted so that you can gain acute insights, which may enable you to score many sure points.

You learn how to confront new questions, or types of questions, and to attack them confidently and work out the correct answers.

You note objectives and emphases, and recognize pitfalls and dangers, so that you may make positive educational adjustments.

Moreover, you are kept fully informed in relation to new concepts, methods, practices, and directions in the field.

You discover that you are actually taking the examination all the time: you are preparing for the examination by "taking" an examination, not by reading extraneous and/or supererogatory textbooks.

In short, this PASSBOOK®, used directedly, should be an important factor in helping you to pass your test.

PURCHASING AGENT

DUTIES
Under general supervision, an employee in this class has responsible charge of all purchasing of a wide variety of equipment, material and supplies for a municipality, special district, or a school district. This involves overseeing the various steps involved in the process of competitive bidding and in establishing contractual agreements that lead to the purchasing of equipment, material and supplies. Responsibilities involve reviewing and approving specifications, analyzing bids to ensure that the product meets the standard specification, and interpreting policies, rules, procedures and regulations relating to the purchase of equipment and supplies, and other pertinent laws concerning public purchasing. The exercise of careful judgment is essential as decisions may impact expenditures of large sums of money. Supervision may be exercised over technical and clerical personnel. Responsible for carrying out the purchasing procedures for the procurement of a group of commodities as part of a central purchasing operation. Communicates with vendors and departmental officials on purchasing problems. Receives and reviews purchase requisitions; obtains and analyzes competitive bids from vendors; collects data on current market conditions; processes invoices; supervises clerical workers who assist with purchasing details. Does related work as required.

SCOPE OF THE WRITTEN TEST
The written test will be designed to cover knowledge, skills, and/or abilities in the
1. **Principles and practices of purchasing** - These questions test for candidates' knowledge of the principles guiding governmental purchasing operations and the ability to put them into practice. These questions may deal with but are not necessarily limited to such matters as the analysis of bids, the use of specifications, the award of contracts, the analysis of market factors that can affect the cost of a purchase, and the application of a set of rules to determine how to proceed with a purchase. Some arithmetic computation may be necessary. No specific knowledge of purchasing laws, rules and regulations will be required to answer these questions.
2. **Preparing written material** - These questions test for the ability to present information clearly and accurately, and to organize paragraphs logically and comprehensibly. For some questions, you will be given information in two or three sentences followed by four restatements of the information. You must then choose the best version. For other questions, you will be given paragraphs with their sentences out of order. You must then choose, from four suggestions, the best order for the sentences.
3. **Supervision** - These questions test for knowledge of the principles and practices employed in planning, organizing, and controlling the activities of a work unit toward predetermined objectives. The concepts covered, usually in a situational question format, include such topics as assigning and reviewing work; evaluating performance; maintaining work standards; motivating and developing subordinates; implementing procedural change; increasing efficiency; and dealing with problems of absenteeism, morale, and discipline.
4. **Understanding and interpreting written material** - These questions test how well you comprehend written material. You will be provided with brief reading selections and will be asked questions about the selections. All the information required to answer the questions will be presented in the selections; you will not be required to have any special knowledge relating to the subject areas of the selections.

HOW TO TAKE A TEST

I. YOU MUST PASS AN EXAMINATION

A. WHAT EVERY CANDIDATE SHOULD KNOW

Examination applicants often ask us for help in preparing for the written test. What can I study in advance? What kinds of questions will be asked? How will the test be given? How will the papers be graded?

As an applicant for a civil service examination, you may be wondering about some of these things. Our purpose here is to suggest effective methods of advance study and to describe civil service examinations.

Your chances for success on this examination can be increased if you know how to prepare. Those "pre-examination jitters" can be reduced if you know what to expect. You can even experience an adventure in good citizenship if you know why civil service exams are given.

B. WHY ARE CIVIL SERVICE EXAMINATIONS GIVEN?

Civil service examinations are important to you in two ways. As a citizen, you want public jobs filled by employees who know how to do their work. As a job seeker, you want a fair chance to compete for that job on an equal footing with other candidates. The best-known means of accomplishing this two-fold goal is the competitive examination.

Exams are widely publicized throughout the nation. They may be administered for jobs in federal, state, city, municipal, town or village governments or agencies.

Any citizen may apply, with some limitations, such as the age or residence of applicants. Your experience and education may be reviewed to see whether you meet the requirements for the particular examination. When these requirements exist, they are reasonable and applied consistently to all applicants. Thus, a competitive examination may cause you some uneasiness now, but it is your privilege and safeguard.

C. HOW ARE CIVIL SERVICE EXAMS DEVELOPED?

Examinations are carefully written by trained technicians who are specialists in the field known as "psychological measurement," in consultation with recognized authorities in the field of work that the test will cover. These experts recommend the subject matter areas or skills to be tested; only those knowledges or skills important to your success on the job are included. The most reliable books and source materials available are used as references. Together, the experts and technicians judge the difficulty level of the questions.

Test technicians know how to phrase questions so that the problem is clearly stated. Their ethics do not permit "trick" or "catch" questions. Questions may have been tried out on sample groups, or subjected to statistical analysis, to determine their usefulness.

Written tests are often used in combination with performance tests, ratings of training and experience, and oral interviews. All of these measures combine to form the best-known means of finding the right person for the right job.

II. HOW TO PASS THE WRITTEN TEST

A. NATURE OF THE EXAMINATION

To prepare intelligently for civil service examinations, you should know how they differ from school examinations you have taken. In school you were assigned certain definite pages to read or subjects to cover. The examination questions were quite detailed and usually emphasized memory. Civil service exams, on the other hand, try to discover your present ability to perform the duties of a position, plus your potentiality to learn these duties. In other words, a civil service exam attempts to predict how successful you will be. Questions cover such a broad area that they cannot be as minute and detailed as school exam questions.

In the public service similar kinds of work, or positions, are grouped together in one "class." This process is known as *position-classification*. All the positions in a class are paid according to the salary range for that class. One class title covers all of these positions, and they are all tested by the same examination.

B. FOUR BASIC STEPS

1) Study the announcement

How, then, can you know what subjects to study? Our best answer is: "Learn as much as possible about the class of positions for which you've applied." The exam will test the knowledge, skills and abilities needed to do the work.

Your most valuable source of information about the position you want is the official exam announcement. This announcement lists the training and experience qualifications. Check these standards and apply only if you come reasonably close to meeting them.

The brief description of the position in the examination announcement offers some clues to the subjects which will be tested. Think about the job itself. Review the duties in your mind. Can you perform them, or are there some in which you are rusty? Fill in the blank spots in your preparation.

Many jurisdictions preview the written test in the exam announcement by including a section called "Knowledge and Abilities Required," "Scope of the Examination," or some similar heading. Here you will find out specifically what fields will be tested.

2) Review your own background

Once you learn in general what the position is all about, and what you need to know to do the work, ask yourself which subjects you already know fairly well and which need improvement. You may wonder whether to concentrate on improving your strong areas or on building some background in your fields of weakness. When the announcement has specified "some knowledge" or "considerable knowledge," or has used adjectives like "beginning principles of…" or "advanced … methods," you can get a clue as to the number and difficulty of questions to be asked in any given field. More questions, and hence broader coverage, would be included for those subjects which are more important in the work. Now weigh your strengths and weaknesses against the job requirements and prepare accordingly.

3) Determine the level of the position

Another way to tell how intensively you should prepare is to understand the level of the job for which you are applying. Is it the entering level? In other words, is this the position in which beginners in a field of work are hired? Or is it an intermediate or advanced level? Sometimes this is indicated by such words as "Junior" or "Senior" in the class title. Other jurisdictions use Roman numerals to designate the level – Clerk I, Clerk II, for example. The word "Supervisor" sometimes appears in the title. If the level is not indicated by the title, check the description of duties. Will you be working under very close supervision, or will you have responsibility for independent decisions in this work?

4) Choose appropriate study materials

Now that you know the subjects to be examined and the relative amount of each subject to be covered, you can choose suitable study materials. For beginning level jobs, or even advanced ones, if you have a pronounced weakness in some aspect of your training, read a modern, standard textbook in that field. Be sure it is up to date and has general coverage. Such books are normally available at your library, and the librarian will be glad to help you locate one. For entry-level positions, questions of appropriate difficulty are chosen – neither highly advanced questions, nor those too simple. Such questions require careful thought but not advanced training.

If the position for which you are applying is technical or advanced, you will read more advanced, specialized material. If you are already familiar with the basic principles of your field, elementary textbooks would waste your time. Concentrate on advanced textbooks and technical periodicals. Think through the concepts and review difficult problems in your field.

These are all general sources. You can get more ideas on your own initiative, following these leads. For example, training manuals and publications of the government agency which employs workers in your field can be useful, particularly for technical and professional positions. A letter or visit to the government department involved may result in more specific study suggestions, and certainly will provide you with a more definite idea of the exact nature of the position you are seeking.

III. KINDS OF TESTS

Tests are used for purposes other than measuring knowledge and ability to perform specified duties. For some positions, it is equally important to test ability to make adjustments to new situations or to profit from training. In others, basic mental abilities not dependent on information are essential. Questions which test these things may not appear as pertinent to the duties of the position as those which test for knowledge and information. Yet they are often highly important parts of a fair examination. For very general questions, it is almost impossible to help you direct your study efforts. What we can do is to point out some of the more common of these general abilities needed in public service positions and describe some typical questions.

1) General information

Broad, general information has been found useful for predicting job success in some kinds of work. This is tested in a variety of ways, from vocabulary lists to questions about current events. Basic background in some field of work, such as sociology or economics, may be sampled in a group of questions. Often these are principles which have become familiar to most persons through exposure rather than through formal training. It is difficult to advise you how to study for these questions; being alert to the world around you is our best suggestion.

2) Verbal ability

An example of an ability needed in many positions is verbal or language ability. Verbal ability is, in brief, the ability to use and understand words. Vocabulary and grammar tests are typical measures of this ability. Reading comprehension or paragraph interpretation questions are common in many kinds of civil service tests. You are given a paragraph of written material and asked to find its central meaning.

3) Numerical ability

Number skills can be tested by the familiar arithmetic problem, by checking paired lists of numbers to see which are alike and which are different, or by interpreting charts and graphs. In the latter test, a graph may be printed in the test booklet which you are asked to use as the basis for answering questions.

4) Observation

A popular test for law-enforcement positions is the observation test. A picture is shown to you for several minutes, then taken away. Questions about the picture test your ability to observe both details and larger elements.

5) Following directions

In many positions in the public service, the employee must be able to carry out written instructions dependably and accurately. You may be given a chart with several columns, each column listing a variety of information. The questions require you to carry out directions involving the information given in the chart.

6) Skills and aptitudes

Performance tests effectively measure some manual skills and aptitudes. When the skill is one in which you are trained, such as typing or shorthand, you can practice. These tests are often very much like those given in business school or high school courses. For many of the other skills and aptitudes, however, no short-time preparation can be made. Skills and abilities natural to you or that you have developed throughout your lifetime are being tested.

Many of the general questions just described provide all the data needed to answer the questions and ask you to use your reasoning ability to find the answers. Your best preparation for these tests, as well as for tests of facts and ideas, is to be at your physical and mental best. You, no doubt, have your own methods of getting into an exam-taking mood and keeping "in shape." The next section lists some ideas on this subject.

IV. KINDS OF QUESTIONS

Only rarely is the "essay" question, which you answer in narrative form, used in civil service tests. Civil service tests are usually of the short-answer type. Full instructions for answering these questions will be given to you at the examination. But in case this is your first experience with short-answer questions and separate answer sheets, here is what you need to know:

1) Multiple-choice Questions

Most popular of the short-answer questions is the "multiple choice" or "best answer" question. It can be used, for example, to test for factual knowledge, ability to solve problems or judgment in meeting situations found at work.

A multiple-choice question is normally one of three types—

- It can begin with an incomplete statement followed by several possible endings. You are to find the one ending which *best* completes the statement, although some of the others may not be entirely wrong.
- It can also be a complete statement in the form of a question which is answered by choosing one of the statements listed.

- It can be in the form of a problem – again you select the best answer.

Here is an example of a multiple-choice question with a discussion which should give you some clues as to the method for choosing the right answer:

When an employee has a complaint about his assignment, the action which will *best* help him overcome his difficulty is to
    A. discuss his difficulty with his coworkers
    B. take the problem to the head of the organization
    C. take the problem to the person who gave him the assignment
    D. say nothing to anyone about his complaint

In answering this question, you should study each of the choices to find which is best. Consider choice "A" – Certainly an employee may discuss his complaint with fellow employees, but no change or improvement can result, and the complaint remains unresolved. Choice "B" is a poor choice since the head of the organization probably does not know what assignment you have been given, and taking your problem to him is known as "going over the head" of the supervisor. The supervisor, or person who made the assignment, is the person who can clarify it or correct any injustice. Choice "C" is, therefore, correct. To say nothing, as in choice "D," is unwise. Supervisors have and interest in knowing the problems employees are facing, and the employee is seeking a solution to his problem.

2) True/False Questions

The "true/false" or "right/wrong" form of question is sometimes used. Here a complete statement is given. Your job is to decide whether the statement is right or wrong.

SAMPLE: A roaming cell-phone call to a nearby city costs less than a non-roaming call to a distant city.

This statement is wrong, or false, since roaming calls are more expensive.
This is not a complete list of all possible question forms, although most of the others are variations of these common types. You will always get complete directions for answering questions. Be sure you understand *how* to mark your answers – ask questions until you do.

V. RECORDING YOUR ANSWERS

Computer terminals are used more and more today for many different kinds of exams.
For an examination with very few applicants, you may be told to record your answers in the test booklet itself. Separate answer sheets are much more common. If this separate answer sheet is to be scored by machine – and this is often the case – it is highly important that you mark your answers correctly in order to get credit.
An electronic scoring machine is often used in civil service offices because of the speed with which papers can be scored. Machine-scored answer sheets must be marked with a pencil, which will be given to you. This pencil has a high graphite content which responds to the electronic scoring machine. As a matter of fact, stray dots may register as answers, so do not let your pencil rest on the answer sheet while you are pondering the correct answer. Also, if your pencil lead breaks or is otherwise defective, ask for another.

Since the answer sheet will be dropped in a slot in the scoring machine, be careful not to bend the corners or get the paper crumpled.

The answer sheet normally has five vertical columns of numbers, with 30 numbers to a column. These numbers correspond to the question numbers in your test booklet. After each number, going across the page are four or five pairs of dotted lines. These short dotted lines have small letters or numbers above them. The first two pairs may also have a "T" or "F" above the letters. This indicates that the first two pairs only are to be used if the questions are of the true-false type. If the questions are multiple choice, disregard the "T" and "F" and pay attention only to the small letters or numbers.

Answer your questions in the manner of the sample that follows:

32. The largest city in the United States is
   A. Washington, D.C.
   B. New York City
   C. Chicago
   D. Detroit
   E. San Francisco

1) Choose the answer you think is best. (New York City is the largest, so "B" is correct.)
2) Find the row of dotted lines numbered the same as the question you are answering. (Find row number 32)
3) Find the pair of dotted lines corresponding to the answer. (Find the pair of lines under the mark "B.")
4) Make a solid black mark between the dotted lines.

VI. BEFORE THE TEST

Common sense will help you find procedures to follow to get ready for an examination. Too many of us, however, overlook these sensible measures. Indeed, nervousness and fatigue have been found to be the most serious reasons why applicants fail to do their best on civil service tests. Here is a list of reminders:

- Begin your preparation early – Don't wait until the last minute to go scurrying around for books and materials or to find out what the position is all about.
- Prepare continuously – An hour a night for a week is better than an all-night cram session. This has been definitely established. What is more, a night a week for a month will return better dividends than crowding your study into a shorter period of time.
- Locate the place of the exam – You have been sent a notice telling you when and where to report for the examination. If the location is in a different town or otherwise unfamiliar to you, it would be well to inquire the best route and learn something about the building.
- Relax the night before the test – Allow your mind to rest. Do not study at all that night. Plan some mild recreation or diversion; then go to bed early and get a good night's sleep.
- Get up early enough to make a leisurely trip to the place for the test – This way unforeseen events, traffic snarls, unfamiliar buildings, etc. will not upset you.
- Dress comfortably – A written test is not a fashion show. You will be known by number and not by name, so wear something comfortable.

- Leave excess paraphernalia at home – Shopping bags and odd bundles will get in your way. You need bring only the items mentioned in the official notice you received; usually everything you need is provided. Do not bring reference books to the exam. They will only confuse those last minutes and be taken away from you when in the test room.
- Arrive somewhat ahead of time – If because of transportation schedules you must get there very early, bring a newspaper or magazine to take your mind off yourself while waiting.
- Locate the examination room – When you have found the proper room, you will be directed to the seat or part of the room where you will sit. Sometimes you are given a sheet of instructions to read while you are waiting. Do not fill out any forms until you are told to do so; just read them and be prepared.
- Relax and prepare to listen to the instructions
- If you have any physical problem that may keep you from doing your best, be sure to tell the test administrator. If you are sick or in poor health, you really cannot do your best on the exam. You can come back and take the test some other time.

VII. AT THE TEST

The day of the test is here and you have the test booklet in your hand. The temptation to get going is very strong. Caution! There is more to success than knowing the right answers. You must know how to identify your papers and understand variations in the type of short-answer question used in this particular examination. Follow these suggestions for maximum results from your efforts:

1) Cooperate with the monitor
The test administrator has a duty to create a situation in which you can be as much at ease as possible. He will give instructions, tell you when to begin, check to see that you are marking your answer sheet correctly, and so on. He is not there to guard you, although he will see that your competitors do not take unfair advantage. He wants to help you do your best.

2) Listen to all instructions
Don't jump the gun! Wait until you understand all directions. In most civil service tests you get more time than you need to answer the questions. So don't be in a hurry. Read each word of instructions until you clearly understand the meaning. Study the examples, listen to all announcements and follow directions. Ask questions if you do not understand what to do.

3) Identify your papers
Civil service exams are usually identified by number only. You will be assigned a number; you must not put your name on your test papers. Be sure to copy your number correctly. Since more than one exam may be given, copy your exact examination title.

4) Plan your time
Unless you are told that a test is a "speed" or "rate of work" test, speed itself is usually not important. Time enough to answer all the questions will be provided, but this does not mean that you have all day. An overall time limit has been set. Divide the total time (in minutes) by the number of questions to determine the approximate time you have for each question.

5) Do not linger over difficult questions

If you come across a difficult question, mark it with a paper clip (useful to have along) and come back to it when you have been through the booklet. One caution if you do this – be sure to skip a number on your answer sheet as well. Check often to be sure that you have not lost your place and that you are marking in the row numbered the same as the question you are answering.

6) Read the questions

Be sure you know what the question asks! Many capable people are unsuccessful because they failed to *read* the questions correctly.

7) Answer all questions

Unless you have been instructed that a penalty will be deducted for incorrect answers, it is better to guess than to omit a question.

8) Speed tests

It is often better NOT to guess on speed tests. It has been found that on timed tests people are tempted to spend the last few seconds before time is called in marking answers at random – without even reading them – in the hope of picking up a few extra points. To discourage this practice, the instructions may warn you that your score will be "corrected" for guessing. That is, a penalty will be applied. The incorrect answers will be deducted from the correct ones, or some other penalty formula will be used.

9) Review your answers

If you finish before time is called, go back to the questions you guessed or omitted to give them further thought. Review other answers if you have time.

10) Return your test materials

If you are ready to leave before others have finished or time is called, take ALL your materials to the monitor and leave quietly. Never take any test material with you. The monitor can discover whose papers are not complete, and taking a test booklet may be grounds for disqualification.

VIII. EXAMINATION TECHNIQUES

1) Read the general instructions carefully. These are usually printed on the first page of the exam booklet. As a rule, these instructions refer to the timing of the examination; the fact that you should not start work until the signal and must stop work at a signal, etc. If there are any *special* instructions, such as a choice of questions to be answered, make sure that you note this instruction carefully.

2) When you are ready to start work on the examination, that is as soon as the signal has been given, read the instructions to each question booklet, underline any key words or phrases, such as *least, best, outline, describe* and the like. In this way you will tend to answer as requested rather than discover on reviewing your paper that you *listed without describing*, that you selected the *worst* choice rather than the *best* choice, etc.

3) If the examination is of the objective or multiple-choice type – that is, each question will also give a series of possible answers: A, B, C or D, and you are called upon to select the best answer and write the letter next to that answer on your answer paper – it is advisable to start answering each question in turn. There may be anywhere from 50 to 100 such questions in the three or four hours allotted and you can see how much time would be taken if you read through all the questions before beginning to answer any. Furthermore, if you come across a question or group of questions which you know would be difficult to answer, it would undoubtedly affect your handling of all the other questions.

4) If the examination is of the essay type and contains but a few questions, it is a moot point as to whether you should read all the questions before starting to answer any one. Of course, if you are given a choice – say five out of seven and the like – then it is essential to read all the questions so you can eliminate the two that are most difficult. If, however, you are asked to answer all the questions, there may be danger in trying to answer the easiest one first because you may find that you will spend too much time on it. The best technique is to answer the first question, then proceed to the second, etc.

5) Time your answers. Before the exam begins, write down the time it started, then add the time allowed for the examination and write down the time it must be completed, then divide the time available somewhat as follows:
   - If 3-1/2 hours are allowed, that would be 210 minutes. If you have 80 objective-type questions, that would be an average of 2-1/2 minutes per question. Allow yourself no more than 2 minutes per question, or a total of 160 minutes, which will permit about 50 minutes to review.
   - If for the time allotment of 210 minutes there are 7 essay questions to answer, that would average about 30 minutes a question. Give yourself only 25 minutes per question so that you have about 35 minutes to review.

6) The most important instruction is to *read each question* and make sure you know what is wanted. The second most important instruction is to *time yourself properly* so that you answer every question. The third most important instruction is to *answer every question*. Guess if you have to but include something for each question. Remember that you will receive no credit for a blank and will probably receive some credit if you write something in answer to an essay question. If you guess a letter – say "B" for a multiple-choice question – you may have guessed right. If you leave a blank as an answer to a multiple-choice question, the examiners may respect your feelings but it will not add a point to your score. Some exams may penalize you for wrong answers, so in such cases *only*, you may not want to guess unless you have some basis for your answer.

7) Suggestions
   a. Objective-type questions
      1. Examine the question booklet for proper sequence of pages and questions
      2. Read all instructions carefully
      3. Skip any question which seems too difficult; return to it after all other questions have been answered
      4. Apportion your time properly; do not spend too much time on any single question or group of questions

5. Note and underline key words – *all, most, fewest, least, best, worst, same, opposite*, etc.
6. Pay particular attention to negatives
7. Note unusual option, e.g., unduly long, short, complex, different or similar in content to the body of the question
8. Observe the use of "hedging" words – *probably, may, most likely*, etc.
9. Make sure that your answer is put next to the same number as the question
10. Do not second-guess unless you have good reason to believe the second answer is definitely more correct
11. Cross out original answer if you decide another answer is more accurate; do not erase until you are ready to hand your paper in
12. Answer all questions; guess unless instructed otherwise
13. Leave time for review

   b. Essay questions
   1. Read each question carefully
   2. Determine exactly what is wanted. Underline key words or phrases.
   3. Decide on outline or paragraph answer
   4. Include many different points and elements unless asked to develop any one or two points or elements
   5. Show impartiality by giving pros and cons unless directed to select one side only
   6. Make and write down any assumptions you find necessary to answer the questions
   7. Watch your English, grammar, punctuation and choice of words
   8. Time your answers; don't crowd material

8) Answering the essay question

Most essay questions can be answered by framing the specific response around several key words or ideas. Here are a few such key words or ideas:

M's: manpower, materials, methods, money, management
P's: purpose, program, policy, plan, procedure, practice, problems, pitfalls, personnel, public relations

   a. Six basic steps in handling problems:
   1. Preliminary plan and background development
   2. Collect information, data and facts
   3. Analyze and interpret information, data and facts
   4. Analyze and develop solutions as well as make recommendations
   5. Prepare report and sell recommendations
   6. Install recommendations and follow up effectiveness

   b. Pitfalls to avoid
   1. *Taking things for granted* – A statement of the situation does not necessarily imply that each of the elements is necessarily true; for example, a complaint may be invalid and biased so that all that can be taken for granted is that a complaint has been registered

2. *Considering only one side of a situation* – Wherever possible, indicate several alternatives and then point out the reasons you selected the best one
3. *Failing to indicate follow up* – Whenever your answer indicates action on your part, make certain that you will take proper follow-up action to see how successful your recommendations, procedures or actions turn out to be
4. *Taking too long in answering any single question* – Remember to time your answers properly

IX. AFTER THE TEST

Scoring procedures differ in detail among civil service jurisdictions although the general principles are the same. Whether the papers are hand-scored or graded by machine we have described, they are nearly always graded by number. That is, the person who marks the paper knows only the number – never the name – of the applicant. Not until all the papers have been graded will they be matched with names. If other tests, such as training and experience or oral interview ratings have been given, scores will be combined. Different parts of the examination usually have different weights. For example, the written test might count 60 percent of the final grade, and a rating of training and experience 40 percent. In many jurisdictions, veterans will have a certain number of points added to their grades.

After the final grade has been determined, the names are placed in grade order and an eligible list is established. There are various methods for resolving ties between those who get the same final grade – probably the most common is to place first the name of the person whose application was received first. Job offers are made from the eligible list in the order the names appear on it. You will be notified of your grade and your rank as soon as all these computations have been made. This will be done as rapidly as possible.

People who are found to meet the requirements in the announcement are called "eligibles." Their names are put on a list of eligible candidates. An eligible's chances of getting a job depend on how high he stands on this list and how fast agencies are filling jobs from the list.

When a job is to be filled from a list of eligibles, the agency asks for the names of people on the list of eligibles for that job. When the civil service commission receives this request, it sends to the agency the names of the three people highest on this list. Or, if the job to be filled has specialized requirements, the office sends the agency the names of the top three persons who meet these requirements from the general list.

The appointing officer makes a choice from among the three people whose names were sent to him. If the selected person accepts the appointment, the names of the others are put back on the list to be considered for future openings.

That is the rule in hiring from all kinds of eligible lists, whether they are for typist, carpenter, chemist, or something else. For every vacancy, the appointing officer has his choice of any one of the top three eligibles on the list. This explains why the person whose name is on top of the list sometimes does not get an appointment when some of the persons lower on the list do. If the appointing officer chooses the second or third eligible, the No. 1 eligible does not get a job at once, but stays on the list until he is appointed or the list is terminated.

X. HOW TO PASS THE INTERVIEW TEST

The examination for which you applied requires an oral interview test. You have already taken the written test and you are now being called for the interview test – the final part of the formal examination.

You may think that it is not possible to prepare for an interview test and that there are no procedures to follow during an interview. Our purpose is to point out some things you can do in advance that will help you and some good rules to follow and pitfalls to avoid while you are being interviewed.

What is an interview supposed to test?

The written examination is designed to test the technical knowledge and competence of the candidate; the oral is designed to evaluate intangible qualities, not readily measured otherwise, and to establish a list showing the relative fitness of each candidate – as measured against his competitors – for the position sought. Scoring is not on the basis of "right" and "wrong," but on a sliding scale of values ranging from "not passable" to "outstanding." As a matter of fact, it is possible to achieve a relatively low score without a single "incorrect" answer because of evident weakness in the qualities being measured.

Occasionally, an examination may consist entirely of an oral test – either an individual or a group oral. In such cases, information is sought concerning the technical knowledges and abilities of the candidate, since there has been no written examination for this purpose. More commonly, however, an oral test is used to supplement a written examination.

Who conducts interviews?

The composition of oral boards varies among different jurisdictions. In nearly all, a representative of the personnel department serves as chairman. One of the members of the board may be a representative of the department in which the candidate would work. In some cases, "outside experts" are used, and, frequently, a businessman or some other representative of the general public is asked to serve. Labor and management or other special groups may be represented. The aim is to secure the services of experts in the appropriate field.

However the board is composed, it is a good idea (and not at all improper or unethical) to ascertain in advance of the interview who the members are and what groups they represent. When you are introduced to them, you will have some idea of their backgrounds and interests, and at least you will not stutter and stammer over their names.

What should be done before the interview?

While knowledge about the board members is useful and takes some of the surprise element out of the interview, there is other preparation which is more substantive. It *is* possible to prepare for an oral interview – in several ways:

1) Keep a copy of your application and review it carefully before the interview

This may be the only document before the oral board, and the starting point of the interview. Know what education and experience you have listed there, and the sequence and dates of all of it. Sometimes the board will ask you to review the highlights of your experience for them; you should not have to hem and haw doing it.

2) Study the class specification and the examination announcement

Usually, the oral board has one or both of these to guide them. The qualities, characteristics or knowledges required by the position sought are stated in these documents. They offer valuable clues as to the nature of the oral interview. For example, if the job involves supervisory responsibilities, the announcement will usually indicate that knowledge of modern supervisory methods and the qualifications of the candidate as a supervisor will be tested. If so, you can expect such questions, frequently in the form of a hypothetical situation which you are expected to solve. NEVER go into an oral without knowledge of the duties and responsibilities of the job you seek.

3) Think through each qualification required

Try to visualize the kind of questions you would ask if you were a board member. How well could you answer them? Try especially to appraise your own knowledge and background in each area, *measured against the job sought*, and identify any areas in which you are weak. Be critical and realistic – do not flatter yourself.

4) Do some general reading in areas in which you feel you may be weak

For example, if the job involves supervision and your past experience has NOT, some general reading in supervisory methods and practices, particularly in the field of human relations, might be useful. Do NOT study agency procedures or detailed manuals. The oral board will be testing your understanding and capacity, not your memory.

5) Get a good night's sleep and watch your general health and mental attitude

You will want a clear head at the interview. Take care of a cold or any other minor ailment, and of course, no hangovers.

What should be done on the day of the interview?

Now comes the day of the interview itself. Give yourself plenty of time to get there. Plan to arrive somewhat ahead of the scheduled time, particularly if your appointment is in the fore part of the day. If a previous candidate fails to appear, the board might be ready for you a bit early. By early afternoon an oral board is almost invariably behind schedule if there are many candidates, and you may have to wait. Take along a book or magazine to read, or your application to review, but leave any extraneous material in the waiting room when you go in for your interview. In any event, relax and compose yourself.

The matter of dress is important. The board is forming impressions about you – from your experience, your manners, your attitude, and your appearance. Give your personal appearance careful attention. Dress your best, but not your flashiest. Choose conservative, appropriate clothing, and be sure it is immaculate. This is a business interview, and your appearance should indicate that you regard it as such. Besides, being well groomed and properly dressed will help boost your confidence.

Sooner or later, someone will call your name and escort you into the interview room. *This is it.* From here on you are on your own. It is too late for any more preparation. But remember, you asked for this opportunity to prove your fitness, and you are here because your request was granted.

What happens when you go in?

The usual sequence of events will be as follows: The clerk (who is often the board stenographer) will introduce you to the chairman of the oral board, who will introduce you to the other members of the board. Acknowledge the introductions before you sit down. Do not be surprised if you find a microphone facing you or a stenotypist sitting by. Oral interviews are usually recorded in the event of an appeal or other review.

Usually the chairman of the board will open the interview by reviewing the highlights of your education and work experience from your application – primarily for the benefit of the other members of the board, as well as to get the material into the record. Do not interrupt or comment unless there is an error or significant misinterpretation; if that is the case, do not hesitate. But do not quibble about insignificant matters. Also, he will usually ask you some question about your education, experience or your present job – partly to get you to start talking and to establish the interviewing "rapport." He may start the actual questioning, or turn it over to one of the other members. Frequently, each member undertakes the questioning on a particular area, one in which he is perhaps most competent, so you can expect each member to participate in the examination. Because time is limited, you may also expect some rather abrupt switches in the direction the questioning takes, so do not be upset by it. Normally, a board member will not pursue a single line of questioning unless he discovers a particular strength or weakness.

After each member has participated, the chairman will usually ask whether any member has any further questions, then will ask you if you have anything you wish to add. Unless you are expecting this question, it may floor you. Worse, it may start you off on an extended, extemporaneous speech. The board is not usually seeking more information. The question is principally to offer you a last opportunity to present further qualifications or to indicate that you have nothing to add. So, if you feel that a significant qualification or characteristic has been overlooked, it is proper to point it out in a sentence or so. Do not compliment the board on the thoroughness of their examination – they have been sketchy, and you know it. If you wish, merely say, "No thank you, I have nothing further to add." This is a point where you can "talk yourself out" of a good impression or fail to present an important bit of information. Remember, *you close the interview yourself.*

The chairman will then say, "That is all, Mr. _____, thank you." Do not be startled; the interview is over, and quicker than you think. Thank him, gather your belongings and take your leave. Save your sigh of relief for the other side of the door.

How to put your best foot forward

Throughout this entire process, you may feel that the board individually and collectively is trying to pierce your defenses, seek out your hidden weaknesses and embarrass and confuse you. Actually, this is not true. They are obliged to make an appraisal of your qualifications for the job you are seeking, and they want to see you in your best light. Remember, they must interview all candidates and a non-cooperative candidate may become a failure in spite of their best efforts to bring out his qualifications. Here are 15 suggestions that will help you:

1) Be natural – Keep your attitude confident, not cocky

If you are not confident that you can do the job, do not expect the board to be. Do not apologize for your weaknesses, try to bring out your strong points. The board is interested in a positive, not negative, presentation. Cockiness will antagonize any board member and make him wonder if you are covering up a weakness by a false show of strength.

2) Get comfortable, but don't lounge or sprawl

Sit erectly but not stiffly. A careless posture may lead the board to conclude that you are careless in other things, or at least that you are not impressed by the importance of the occasion. Either conclusion is natural, even if incorrect. Do not fuss with your clothing, a pencil or an ashtray. Your hands may occasionally be useful to emphasize a point; do not let them become a point of distraction.

3) Do not wisecrack or make small talk

This is a serious situation, and your attitude should show that you consider it as such. Further, the time of the board is limited – they do not want to waste it, and neither should you.

4) Do not exaggerate your experience or abilities

In the first place, from information in the application or other interviews and sources, the board may know more about you than you think. Secondly, you probably will not get away with it. An experienced board is rather adept at spotting such a situation, so do not take the chance.

5) If you know a board member, do not make a point of it, yet do not hide it

Certainly you are not fooling him, and probably not the other members of the board. Do not try to take advantage of your acquaintanceship – it will probably do you little good.

6) Do not dominate the interview

Let the board do that. They will give you the clues – do not assume that you have to do all the talking. Realize that the board has a number of questions to ask you, and do not try to take up all the interview time by showing off your extensive knowledge of the answer to the first one.

7) Be attentive

You only have 20 minutes or so, and you should keep your attention at its sharpest throughout. When a member is addressing a problem or question to you, give him your undivided attention. Address your reply principally to him, but do not exclude the other board members.

8) Do not interrupt

A board member may be stating a problem for you to analyze. He will ask you a question when the time comes. Let him state the problem, and wait for the question.

9) Make sure you understand the question

Do not try to answer until you are sure what the question is. If it is not clear, restate it in your own words or ask the board member to clarify it for you. However, do not haggle about minor elements.

10) Reply promptly but not hastily

A common entry on oral board rating sheets is "candidate responded readily," or "candidate hesitated in replies." Respond as promptly and quickly as you can, but do not jump to a hasty, ill-considered answer.

11) Do not be peremptory in your answers

A brief answer is proper – but do not fire your answer back. That is a losing game from your point of view. The board member can probably ask questions much faster than you can answer them.

12) Do not try to create the answer you think the board member wants

He is interested in what kind of mind you have and how it works – not in playing games. Furthermore, he can usually spot this practice and will actually grade you down on it.

13) Do not switch sides in your reply merely to agree with a board member

Frequently, a member will take a contrary position merely to draw you out and to see if you are willing and able to defend your point of view. Do not start a debate, yet do not surrender a good position. If a position is worth taking, it is worth defending.

14) Do not be afraid to admit an error in judgment if you are shown to be wrong

The board knows that you are forced to reply without any opportunity for careful consideration. Your answer may be demonstrably wrong. If so, admit it and get on with the interview.

15) Do not dwell at length on your present job

The opening question may relate to your present assignment. Answer the question but do not go into an extended discussion. You are being examined for a *new* job, not your present one. As a matter of fact, try to phrase ALL your answers in terms of the job for which you are being examined.

Basis of Rating

Probably you will forget most of these "do's" and "don'ts" when you walk into the oral interview room. Even remembering them all will not ensure you a passing grade. Perhaps you did not have the qualifications in the first place. But remembering them will help you to put your best foot forward, without treading on the toes of the board members.

Rumor and popular opinion to the contrary notwithstanding, an oral board wants you to make the best appearance possible. They know you are under pressure – but they also want to see how you respond to it as a guide to what your reaction would be under the pressures of the job you seek. They will be influenced by the degree of poise you display, the personal traits you show and the manner in which you respond.

ABOUT THIS BOOK

This book contains tests divided into Examination Sections. Go through each test, answering every question in the margin. We have also attached a sample answer sheet at the back of the book that can be removed and used. At the end of each test look at the answer key and check your answers. On the ones you got wrong, look at the right answer choice and learn. Do not fill in the answers first. Do not memorize the questions and answers, but understand the answer and principles involved. On your test, the questions will likely be different from the samples. Questions are changed and new ones added. If you understand these past questions you should have success with any changes that arise. Tests may consist of several types of questions. We have additional books on each subject should more study be advisable or necessary for you. Finally, the more you study, the better prepared you will be. This book is intended to be the last thing you study before you walk into the examination room. Prior study of relevant texts is also recommended. NLC publishes some of these in our Fundamental Series. Knowledge and good sense are important factors in passing your exam. Good luck also helps. So now study this Passbook, absorb the material contained within and take that knowledge into the examination. Then do your best to pass that exam.

EXAMINATION SECTION

EXAMINATION SECTION
TEST 1

DIRECTIONS: Each question or incomplete statement is followed by several suggested answers or completions. Select the one the BEST answers the question or completes the statement. *PRINT THE LETTER OF THE CORRECT ANSWER IN THE SPACE AT THE RIGHT.*

1. In submitting a request for bids, a buyer's specifications should be written in a way that 1._____

    A. limits the ranges of tolerance as much as possible
    B. allows more than one supplier to be competitive
    C. allows multiple interpretations of what is desired
    D. guarantees one successful bid

2. An agency commissions a graphic arts firm to design a letterhead and print the official stationery for the agency. In order to insure that the agency itself holds ownership of the design of the letterhead, the buyer should be sure to include a(n) _____ clause in the purchase agreement. 2._____

    A. severability
    B. hold harmless
    C. disclaimer
    D. work for hire

3. After receiving a bid from a supplier, a buyer decides to change some of the terms and conditions of the original request, and makes the changes on the purchase order. The purchase order, in terms of contract law, may now be considered a(n) 3._____

    A. counteroffer
    B. acceptance
    C. offer
    D. consideration

4. A buyer has limited space available for inventory storage, and the supplier's goods are therefore delivered in small batches. To lower the purchasing costs, the buyer should try to 4._____

    A. order from several different suppliers
    B. send a worker from the organization to pick up the supplies, since they are small-batch shipments, to eliminate shipping costs
    C. offer to store inventory on consignment
    D. order larger batches, but spread out delivery until needed and the time for payments at an appropriate interval after each delivery

5. A way bill is a 5._____

    A. fee charged by the common carrier for the transport of goods
    B. list of goods sent by a common carrier with shipping directions
    C. specification of the weight of packaging or wrapping of a product
    D. written receipt given by a carrier for goods accepted for transportation

6. Which of the following methods of shipment is typically MOST expensive? 6.____

   A. Less truck load (LTL)
   B. Less rail carload
   C. Rail carload
   D. Truckload

7. "Budgetary quotations" from vendors 7.____

   A. are long-term projections
   B. do not represent a binding commitment
   C. should not be used at all in making cost estimates
   D. are a good tool for leveraging price reductions during negotiations

8. A supplier requests a price increase of 3% on a long-term materials purchasing agreement. In order to negotiate the request, the buyer should be keeping an accessible record of 8.____
   I. the date(s) of the supplier's last price increase(s) on the materials
   II. how much prices have changed over time for the materials
   III. the cost-of-living adjustment index over the given period of time
   IV. the purchasing organization's change in revenues over the given period of time

   A. I and II
   B. I, II and III
   C. III and IV
   D. I, II, III and IV

9. Each of the following is a reason organizations use purchase orders to document transactions, EXCEPT to 9.____

   A. help control administrative matters
   B. facilitate the management of purchasing functions
   C. eliminate the need to look up price histories
   D. provide legal protection for the buying organization

10. A buyer has decided to use sample testing as a quality assessment strategy for a supplier's goods. As a rule, the samples should be tested 10.____

    A. and then destroyed
    B. before they are shipped
    C. without the use of statistical methods
    D. randomly throughout the batch

11. Express warranties include each of the following, EXCEPT a supplier's 11.____

    A. unstated promise that the product is fit for the ordinary purposes for which it is used
    B. oral or written promise containing representations that the product is defect free and/or a promise to repair or replace it.
    C. written promise to repair or replace defective parts for a stated period of time. This is a typical Song Beverly express warranty.
    D. written promise or affirmation of fact which describes the product at the time of sale

12. A seller offers a buyer a discount that is stipulated "2 percent 10th prox." on the purchase order. This means that the buyer will receive the 2 percent discount if the invoice is paid

    A. within ten days
    B. before the end of the month
    C. on or before the 10th of the following month
    D. within six months

12.____

13. The _____ department at the buying organization typically checks to make certain the products received match the specifications of what was ordered and reports discrepancies.

    A. quality control   B. accounting
    C. purchasing   D. receiving

13.____

14. When carrying out the purchasing function, a buyer should think of the _____ as the customer.

    A. buyer himself/herself
    B. purchasing department
    C. purchasing organization that is paying for the product
    D. requestor or user of the product purchased

14.____

15. For most organizations, a _____ supply of commonly-used business forms is considered optimal, taking all factors into account.

    A. monthly   B. quarterly   C. six-month   D. yearly

15.____

16. The most commonly used term indicating the geographical point where ownership passes from the seller to the buyer is

    A. Free On Board   B. Duty-free
    C. Free Along Side   D. Point of Assumption

16.____

17. Ideally-except for unique items available only from one supplier-competitive quotations should be obtained

    A. every time an order is placed
    B. every six months
    C. annually
    D. every two years

17.____

18. The F.O.B. point specified in a purchase order determines

    A. the cost of insurance and freight during delivery
    B. the means by which purchased goods are transported
    C. who normally pays for transportation of purchased goods
    D. whether the purchased goods have been paid for

18.____

19. The object of a(n) _____ bill of lading is to enable a shipper to collect for his shipment before it reaches destination.

    A. order
    B. straight
    C. export
    D. foul

20. What is the term for an invoice sent by a supplier in advance of the actual sale for planning or other purposes?

    A. Traveler card
    B. Release
    C. Tickler
    D. Pro forma

21. When a purchasing agent arranges an order for long-term material needs, he should be sure to require a(n)

    A. flexible specification
    B. hold harmless clause
    C. supremacy clause
    D. sample shipment

22. In order to ensure prompt delivery of the material or service specified on a purchase order, a purchaser's best choice is to

    A. write "ASAP" as the delivery date
    B. specify the length of time in terms of days
    C. specify the length of time in terms of weeks
    D. specify the exact date by which the material will be delivered or the service completed

23. Of the categories of purchases used at a mid- to large-sized organization, the LEAST common is

    A. maintenance, repair, and operating supplies
    B. raw material
    C. items for resale
    D. capital equipment

24. A purchasing agent should typically expect to have the LEAST amount of authority in the purchase of

    A. MRO purchases
    B. consulting services
    C. revenue-producing items
    D. capital equipment

25. A buyer arranges a purchase agreement stating that the order will be shipped "C&F destination." This means that the 25.____

    A. supplier arranges for the insurance and charges the buyer
    B. supplier pays the F.O.B. costs
    C. buyer pays for the F.O.B costs
    D. buyer bills the supplier for transportation costs

KEY (CORRECT ANSWERS)

1.	B	11.	A
2.	D	12.	C
3.	A	13.	A
4.	D	14.	D
5.	B	15.	C
6.	A	16.	A
7.	B	17.	C
8.	A	18.	C
9.	C	19.	A
10.	D	20.	D

21.	D
22.	D
23.	C
24.	B
25.	C

TEST 2

DIRECTIONS: Each question or incomplete statement is followed by several suggested answers or completions. Select the one the BEST answers the question or completes the statement. *PRINT THE LETTER OF THE CORRECT ANSWER IN THE SPACE AT THE RIGHT.*

1. The Last In First Out (LIFO) accounting method 1.____
    I. values inventory at current prices
    II. tends to postpone outlays for income taxes
    III. shows higher income than First In First Out (FIFO) if prices are rising

    A. I only
    B. I and II
    C. I and III
    D. II and III

2. Which of the following is an express warranty? 2.____

    A. "The delivered product will match the physical dimensions of the submitted sample."
    B. "This is the best computer available on the market today."
    C. "This truck gets great gas mileage."
    D. "I guarantee you'll be satisfied with this printer."

3. For routine supplies that are widely available, the most important purchasing cost factor, other than price, is probably 3.____

    A. required delivery date
    B. labor charges
    C. material quality
    D. shipping charges

4. Which of the following is a term frequently used in connection with bills of lading which are endorsed over to another party by the owner of the bill-giving the party named the title to the property covered by the bill of lading? 4.____

    A. Pledge
    B. Assignment
    C. Attachment
    D. Transference

5. A buyer writes "ASAP" on a purchase order in order to communicate the urgency of the supplier's delivery. The main problem with this approach is that it 5.____

    A. communicates a lack of planning and discipline on the part of the buyer's organization
    B. puts pressure on the supplier to meet an unrealistic deadline
    C. does not specify a specific date for delivery
    D. is an acronym that has multiple meanings

6. A supplier has negotiated "net terms" for a purchase. This means that

   A. the supplier's invoice must be paid without discount on or before the due date
   B. the buyer will only pay for what is delivered, when it is delivered
   C. the supplier will offer a discount if the buyer pays an invoice before the due date
   D. the buyer pays for everything up front

7. A company has purchased a machine for making envelopes. A week after it is put into operation, a bolt in the machine is sheared off and the broken end is flung several feet, injuring a worker in the eye. In order to arrange an agreement in which the supplier would assume liability for this injury, a buyer would probably have to delete the existing exclusion concerning

   A. consequential damages
   B. negotiable instruments
   C. implied warranty
   D. unconscionability

8. _____ is a term of quality concern that usually involves pre-packaged, off-the-shelf items.

   A. Planned obsolescence
   B. In-process checking
   C. Concealed discrepancy
   D. Tare deduction

9. Which of the following is an advantage typically associated with the use of procurement cards among an organization's employees?

   A. Tight control over number and type of purchases
   B. Lower overall cost of the purchasing function
   C. Strengthened negotiating position
   D. Savings in paperwork and time

10. The theory of "first bid, final bid" is that
    I. a supplier will keep the price as low as possible
    II. a supplier will make the terms as favorable as possible
    III. the buyer will save time
    IV. the buyer will have maximum flexibility in choosing terms and price

    A. I and II
    B. I, II and III
    C. II and IV
    D. I, II, III and IV

11. An implied warranty of merchantability is the implicit promise that a product will be

    A. fit for the ordinary purposes for which it is used
    B. similar or identical to the products of its competitors
    C. fit for the particular purpose specified by the buyer
    D. repaired or replaced, if defective, within a reasonable period of time

12. The price of a product is $45. The supplier wants to increase the price to $50, but the purchasing agent convinces the supplier to keep the price the same. The percentage saved by the agent was

    A. 10
    B. 11.1
    C. 15
    D. 22.33

13. A buyer for a local government office purchases Brand X paint for the building's interior rooms at the lowest available price, which is $5 a gallon less than the nearest competitor, Brand A. Which of the following, if true, would have been a legitimate reason for the buyer to decide on buying Brand A?

    A. The agency only planned to occupy the building for a year or so
    B. The application of Brand A costs slightly more than applying Brand X
    C. Other agencies have used Brand A for their offices and have had no complaints
    D. Brand A is twice as durable as Brand X

14. "External lead-time" includes the time required for the
    I. supplier to manufacture the ordered material
    II. carrier to transport the ordered material
    III. purchaser to inspect the quality of the goods upon arrival
    IV. purchaser to deliver the material to the requestor

    A. I only
    B. I and II
    C. III and IV
    D. I, II, III and IV

15. The portion of law that is concerned with the scope of a buyer's or purchaser's authority is known as the Law of

    A. Agency
    B. Torts
    C. Contract
    D. Partnership

16. Inputs into a material requirements planning (MRP) system include each of the following, EXCEPT

    A. holding costs
    B. lead times
    C. bills of materials
    D. production schedule

17. Often, a long-term agreement between a buyer and supplier does not specify on the purchase order form what quantity to ship at any one time, or the dates that shipment should be made. The mechanism for ordering in this type of arrangement is the

    A. invoice
    B. release form
    C. traveler card
    D. pro forma

18. Most of the disputes concerning orders for long-term material needs arise because   18.____

   A. turnover at the supplier's workplace is high
   B. manufacturing standards constantly evolve
   C. the definition of acceptability is too vague
   D. the purchasing organization hasn't maintained adequate records

19. For a purchasing company that is experiencing habitually late shipments from its suppliers, the least costly solution is likely to be   19.____

   A. ordering material from multiple suppliers
   B. carrying high inventory
   C. multiple follow-ups with a supplier or shipper
   D. implementing a just-in-time purchasing arrangement

20. To gain a price reduction from a supplier, a purchasing agent's FIRST step should be to   20.____

   A. threaten to change suppliers
   B. offer to pay cash
   C. offer to accept a later delivery schedule
   D. ask the supplier to lower the price

21. The _____ department at the buying organization typically matches invoices to the purchase order to make certain that prices, terms, and the quantities and items received agree before payment is approved.   21.____

   A. purchasing   B. receiving
   C. quality control   D. accounting

22. For _____, the best purchasing approach is usually to keep as little as possible on hand.   22.____

   A. revenue-producing items
   B. office supplies
   C. capital expenditures
   D. printed forms

23. In international trade, a seller often agrees to deliver the product to a specified port for ocean shipping. Afterwards the buyer pays for the cost of loading, marine insurance, and further transportation costs. This type of agreement is described as   23.____

   A. Forward Buying   B. Tare Free
   C. Free Along Side   D. Free On Board

24. An Economic Order Quantity (EOQ) formula would be an appropriate inventory method for   24.____

   A. consulting services   B. machines used in production
   C. office supplies   D. fleet vehicles

25. Relative to financing a purchase, leasing typically has the advantage of
   I.   greater flexibility
   II. fewer financial restrictions
   III. lower overall costs
   IV. full control over the leased item

   A. I and II
   B. I, II and III
   C. II and III
   D. I, II, III and IV

KEY (CORRECT ANSWERS)

1.	B	11.	A
2.	A	12.	B
3.	A	13.	D
4.	B	14.	B
5.	C	15.	A
6.	A	16.	A
7.	A	17.	B
8.	C	18.	C
9.	D	19.	D
10.	B	20.	D

21.	D
22.	A
23.	C
24.	C
25.	A

EXAMINATION SECTION
TEST 1

DIRECTIONS: Each question or incomplete statement is followed by several suggested answers or completions. Select the one the BEST answers the question or completes the statement. *PRINT THE LETTER OF THE CORRECT ANSWER IN THE SPACE AT THE RIGHT.*

1. A purchase order must include the
   - I. name and address of the supplier
   - II. payment terms
   - III. quantity of goods/services purchases
   - IV. location where the buyer will take ownership

   A. I and III
   B. I, II and III
   C. II and III
   D. I, II, III and IV

   1.____

2. Typically, ownership referred to as "title of goods" is transferred from seller to buyer when

   A. initial payment for the goods has been made
   B. the goods are transferred from seller to buyer at the agreed-upon point of delivery
   C. final payment for the goods has been made
   D. the title document is delivered to the buyer from the seller

   2.____

3. Team-buying arrangements are usually MOST appropriate for transactions that are

   A. low-value and routine
   B. low-value and one-time
   C. high-value and one-time
   D. high-value and continuous

   3.____

4. A(n) _____ bill of lading is a nonnegotiable document and provides that a shipment is to be delivered direct to the party whose name is shown as consignee.

   A. foul
   B. straight
   C. order
   D. clean

   4.____

5. What is the term for the process of notifying a buyer that an offer or purchase order has been received?

   A. Exchange
   B. Consideration
   C. Substantiation
   D. Acknowledgement

   5.____

6. Effective methods of cutting down on office supply expenses generally include
   I. standardizing products
   II. allow sales personnel to call on each office employee individually to determine need
   III. use a systems contract
   IV. have supplies located at several different locations throughout the workplace

   A. I only
   B. I and III
   C. II, III and IV
   D. IV only

7. A seller offers a buyer a discount that is stipulated "2 percent 1-60X" on the purchase order. This means the buyer will receive the 2 percent discount if the invoice is paid within _____ days of the delivery date.

   A. 60
   B. 70
   C. 90
   D. 121

8. A business that transports goods by motor vehicle to a customer and agrees to accept certain terms and conditions is known specifically as a

   A. contract carrier
   B. freight company
   C. common carrier
   D. bailor

9. A "traveler card" in a purchasing office is a type of

   A. purchase order
   B. price history
   C. release form
   D. requisition fo

10. In evaluating the quality of a vendor, the most important factor is probably

    A. whether the vendor prefers a purchase order or a contract
    B. how the vendor reacts to problems
    C. price
    D. an absence of problems

11. Probably the most important factor in the success of purchasing efforts is the

    A. clarity of delivery date
    B. lead-time involved
    C. calculation of price
    D. quality of specifications

12. Buyers at an organization are normally considered to be _____ purchasing agents.

    A. universal   B. general   C. principal   D. special

13. In order to function more smoothly with other departments in an organization, such as receiving, purchasing should network its computer system. Usually, it would be appropriate for receiving to have access to information about each of the following, EXCEPT

    A. delivery dates
    B. price information
    C. F.O.B. points
    D. invoice dates

14. "Safety stock" is added inventory that is meant to insure against each of the following, EXCEPT

    A. a sales bubble
    B. unexpected lead time
    C. fluctuating rates of usage
    D. obsolescence, failure, or breakage

15. For a printing project, the most efficient way to specify the organization's needs is to

    A. rely on standard procedures
    B. request a number of samples
    C. provide a sample
    D. provide a bulleted list of extremely narrow requirements

16. In larger organizations, the _____ is usually established outside of the purchasing operation.

    A. request for bids
    B. request for bids
    C. maximum price
    D. need for materials or services
    E. confirmation of orders

17. Which of the following methods of shipment is typically LEAST expensive?

    A. Truckload
    B. Rail carload
    C. Less truckload (LTL)
    D. Less carload

18. What is the term for the document used on foreign trade that requires payment by the seller's bank for a shipment when the document is presented and accompanied by any agreed-upon proof of shipment?

    A. FOB
    B. Letter of credit
    C. Pro forma
    D. Sight draft

19. The most appropriate office software for bid analysis is the

    A. slide presentation
    B. expert system
    C. spreadsheet
    D. financial planner

20. For a buyer, the first step in quality assurance is usually

    A. making a thorough inspection of a product as soon as it is shipped
    B. communicating the importance of meeting the given standards
    C. obtaining a variety of samples
    D. writing good specifications

21. Items that are used internally in a business or organization are often abbreviated _____ on purchasing documents.

    A. ISO
    B. FOB
    C. LCL
    D. MRO

22. The economic order quantity (EOQ) of an item depends on each of the following factors, EXCEPT

    A. unit demand
    B. quantity price breaks
    C. holding costs
    D. costs of being out of inventory

23. Which of the following is most clearly a breach of the implied warranty of fitness for a particular purpose?

    A. The lead of a pencil, just delivered by a supplier, breaks every time an office worker puts it to paper.
    B. The paint that a buyer recently purchased, one month after being properly applied by a contractor, is peeling from the walls.
    C. A metal machine component is .025 of an inch longer than allowed by the specifications of a purchase order.
    D. Reams of paper delivered by the supplier are slightly too large to fit into the paper tray of the copy machine for which they were intended.

24. A supplier tries to change the terms of an agreement at the last minute by adjusting the price upward. The buyer's right to _____ allows him to purchase goods from another source and obtain any difference in price from the original supplier.

    A. cover
    B. exemption
    C. recourse
    D. utility

25. A retail store sells equal amounts of a product over a five-month period, beginning in January, at a 100% markup. The company's annual interest rate is 10 percent. The most efficient purchasing structure would be to

    A. buy all the products up front in a lump purchase
    B. use weekly sales to predict quantity, and then place orders
    C. spread purchases out in five equal monthly amounts
    D. buy all the products up front in a lump purchase, but divide the deliv-

25.____

KEY (CORRECT ANSWERS)

1.	D	11.	D
2.	B	12.	B
3.	D	13.	B
4.	B	14.	D
5.	D	15.	C
6.	B	16.	C
7.	B	17.	B
8.	A	18.	D
9.	D	19.	C
10.	B	20.	B

    21. D
    22. B
    23. B
    24. A
    25. D

TEST 2

DIRECTIONS: Each question or incomplete statement is followed by several suggested answers or completions. Select the one the BEST answers the question or completes the statement. *PRINT THE LETTER OF THE CORRECT ANSWER IN THE SPACE AT THE RIGHT.*

1. In predicting prices, a buyer should rely LEAST on   1.____

    A. trends
    B. budgets
    C. vendor communication
    D. experience

2. The main advantage of an operating lease is that it   2.____

    A. can be converted into ownership cheaply and quickly
    B. does not have to be entered on the balance sheet as a liability
    C. they are inherently unstructured
    D. reduces overall acquisition costs

3. The Economic Order Quantity formula takes each of the following into account, EXCEPT   3.____

    A. price
    B. obsolescence
    C. the holding cost of inventory
    D. the cost of placing an order

4. A purchasing agent's activity report will usually contain each of the following, EXCEPT   4.____

    A. impending strikes
    B. major price increases or reductions
    C. current lead times for certain items
    D. unresolved claims for damaged material

5. The bill of lading is a   5.____

    A. written receipt given by a carrier for goods accepted for transportation
    B. fee charged by a government for certain goods brought into the country
    C. purchase order for materials or supplies used over an extended period of time
    D. list of goods sent by a common carrier with shipping directions

6. Which of the following federal agencies compiles the Producer Price Index (PPI)?   6.____

    A. Small Business Administration
    B. Bureau of Economic Analysis
    C. Bureau of Labor Statistics
    D. Patent and Trademark Office

7. A request for quotation (RFQ) should   7.____
    I. give the names of all competitors
    II. avoid language such as "evaluate the feasibility" or "reserves the right to"
    III. identify the estimated annual purchases of the expense category
    IV. always be in writing

A. I and III
B. II and III
C. II, III and IV
D. I, II, III and IV

8. Probably the major reason for failed negotiations with a potential supplier is that the buyer

   A. doesn't allow sufficient time to reach an agreement
   B. technology changes rapidly
   C. isn't willing to offer endorsements up-front
   D. has not adequately planned for negotiations

9. Sellers may disclaim the implied warranty of merchantability by using the
   I. word "merchantability" in the disclaimer, and writing the disclaimer itself conspicuously (in larger type or ALL CAPITALS, etc.)
   II. phrase "as is"
   III. phrase "with all faults"
   IV. phrase "not for resale"

   A. I and II
   B. I, II and III
   C. II and III
   D. I, II, III and IV

10. For a buyer, the most accurate way to think of "price" would be to view it as

    A. the final determining factor in all purchasing decisions
    B. a dependent variable that changes in relation to factors such as delivery time, quality, and warranties
    C. one component of cost, but not necessarily the most important
    D. a margin over cost that is passed on to the purchasing company's customers

11. "Dating" is a method of

    A. granting extended credit terms used by sellers to induce buyers to receive goods in advance of their required delivery date, thus permitting the seller to ship goods earlier than the buyer would ordinarily wish to receive them
    B. stipulating that the price of the goods ordered is subject to change at the vendor's discretion between the date the order is placed and the date the vendor makes shipment, and that the then established price is the contract price
    C. debiting delays in excess of the allowed free time provided in tariffs against the consignor (or consignee), and crediting delays less than those allowed to the consignor (or consignee)
    D. withholding a portion of the sum due a vendor until the purchase has been finally accepted as fully meeting specifications

12. A buyer has a relationship with a supplier that is on an order-by-order basis, with no special provisions about price increases in the contract. The supplier announces a price increase. The buyer knows that the cost of switching to another supplier will probably equal, if not exceed, the cost of the price increase. The buyer should

A. threaten to open the contract up for competitive bidding
B. offer to buy a larger quantity of items in order to lower the price
C. ask the supplier for a 90-day postponement for budget adjustment
D. threaten to make a contract with the supplier's leading competitor

13. In analyzing a group of bids, a buyer's should think of his/her primary responsibility as   13._____

    A. locating hidden costs
    B. finding the lowest possible price
    C. converting price information into cost information
    D. avoiding any kind of risk

14. In negotiation with a supplier, a buyer for Agency X makes the statement that Agency X   14._____
    is already receiving a product offered by a supplier for a lower price from another supplier. The supplier challenges the buyer's statement in court, and the buyer is unable to prove that his statement was correct. The buyer is in violation of _____ law.

    A. labor
    B. false advertising
    C. antitrust
    D. trade secrecy

15. Which of the following terms is synonymous with "equity?"   15._____

    A. Book value
    B. Deferred revenue
    C. Asset turnover
    D. Future value

16. Hard copies of bills of material usually include   16._____
    I. the name of the supplier
    II. the quantity needed
    III. the price previously paid for the material
    IV. a brief description of the item needed

    A. I and II
    B. I, II and III
    C. II and IV
    D. I, II, III and IV

17. A buyer wants to ensure that quality assurance is an issue that is important to a supplier.   17._____
    Before the buyer even enters into an agreement with a supplier, the best way to do this would be to

    A. write very narrow specifications
    B. request a description of the supplier's own quality assurance policies and protocols
    C. reiterate several times, on several occasions, that quality assurance is important to the long-term life of the purchasing agreement
    D. make a list of qualities or characteristics that will be considered unacceptable

18. In order for a contract to be legal,
    I.   the agreement must involve legal subject matter
    II. there must be an offer
    III. there must be an acceptance
    IV. parties to the agreement must be capable

    A. I and III
    B. I, II and III
    C. II, III and IV
    D. I, II, III and IV

19. A buyer issues a purchase order for certain office supplies at a certain price that she believes was agreed upon by the supplier. The supplier does not agree with the price that is listed on the purchase order. Under contract law, the supplier has a period of _____ days from the receipt of the written purchase order to voice an objection.

    A. 5
    B. 10
    C. 30
    D. 60

20. The "Just in Time" ordering method is best suited to organizations that

    A. provide services that are dependent on the prompt arrival of certain supplies
    B. have sales marked by pronounced boom-and-bust cycles
    C. works with informal procedures
    D. use standard products on a continual basis for an extended period of time

21. The _____ department at the buying organization typically compares purchase order items and quantities with the physical items received and reports any discrepancies.

    A. accounting
    B. receiving
    C. purchasing
    D. quality control

22. Advantages of multiple sourcing include
    I.   less time spent on the purchasing function
    II. overall cost reduction
    III. protection against poor performance by a supplier
    IV. flexible specifications

    A. I and II
    B. II, III and IV
    C. III only
    D. I, II, III and IV

23. Many buyers try to ensure the success of a purchasing agreement by writing specifications that are as narrow as possible. The greatest risk associated with this strategy is that

    A. it nearly always results in added fees or charges
    B. the availability of the named items may be limited
    C. the item is often too narrowly defined to fit the intended purpose
    D. other products that may satisfy the need at lower cost are excluded

24. A purchasing agent orders a list of supplies from a large producer of metal products. The purchase includes several pressed metal sheets that will be used in manufacturing parts for resale. The supplier's invoice includes the same rate of sales tax for all the goods listed on the invoice. The purchasing agent should know that

 A. before the sheets can be purchased, they must be approved by the CPSC
 B. most states do not apply sales taxes to raw materials used in the manufacture of products for resale.
 C. the transformation of the metal sheets into a final product will require certain skills and machinery
 D. it is the purchasing organization's responsibility to ensure that the metal sheets are produced under OSHA-approved conditions

24.____

25. "Consideration" is a term in contract law that refers to the

 A. process of notifying a buyer that an offer or purchase order has been received
 B. careful inspection of the words of a contract, to make sure it says what each party wants it to
 C. giving of something-usually money-in exchange for goods or services
 D. fairness and rightness of conduct or action, given the circumstances

25.____

KEY (CORRECT ANSWERS)

1.	A	11.	A
2.	B	12.	C
3.	B	13.	C
4.	C	14.	C
5.	A	15.	A
6.	C	16.	C
7.	D	17.	B
8.	D	18.	D
9.	B	19.	B
10.	C	20.	D

21. B
22. C
23. D
24. B
25. C

EXAMINATION SECTION
TEST 1

DIRECTIONS: Each question or incomplete statement is followed by several suggested answers or completions. Select the one that BEST answers the question or completes the statement. *PRINT THE LETTER OF THE CORRECT ANSWER IN THE SPACE AT THE RIGHT.*

1. Of the following, the BEST advantage of centralized purchasing is that it is likely to result in

    A. lower unit costs of commodities
    B. a reduction in the number of personnel devoting time to purchasing
    C. more suppliers selling their commodities to the city
    D. less standardization of items used by the various city agencies

    1._____

2. All of the following are characteristics of a representative specification EXCEPT that the

    A. required quality is described clearly
    B. industry standards are utilized wherever possible
    C. criteria for testing upon delivery of goods are clearly described
    D. tolerances are drawn closer than those in industry standards to assure compliance with the specification

    2._____

3. Of the following, it is MOST important for agencies to anticipate their purchase requirements adequately so that the buyer may

    A. have time to search the market for the best value
    B. secure prices for larger quantities of the item needed
    C. have time to search the market for substitutes
    D. have time to search the market for seconds

    3._____

4. The one of the following which is a function of a purchasing procedure manual is to explain to

    A. potential vendors how to sell merchandise to the city
    B. agencies how to negotiate with vendors for their purchasing needs for materials, supplies, and equipment
    C. potential vendors which agencies will use certain commodities
    D. agencies how to request an item to be purchased and how the purchase will be accomplished

    4._____

5. The one of the following items which need NOT be included on a requisition submitted by an agency is the

    A. quality of the item needed
    B. description of the item needed
    C. name of the agency preparing the requisition
    D. name of the vendor from whom the item is to be purchased

    5._____

6. Which one of the following items is NOT a factor to be taken into consideration by a buyer when considering the suitability of a potential source of supply?

    A. Accessibility of the supplier
    B. Financial position of the supplier

    6._____

C. Cash discount items offered by the supplier
D. Reliability of the supplier

7. Which one of the following is the LEAST important reason for a buyer to initiate a purchase?
A(n)

   A. advertisement offers a bargain for a product used occasionally
   B. need for a commodity develops an agency
   C. minimum inventory is reached in a stock item in the storeroom
   D. construction project requires equipment for the completion of a building

8. If an agency requests the purchase of materials for a current renovation project, the LEAST important thing for a buyer to consider in handling this purchase transaction is

   A. quantity requirements
   B. when the materials will be delivered
   C. the kinds of materials required
   D. what type of renovation is being done

9. Acceptance of a sample from a potential supplier carries with it an obligation for the buyer to

   A. return it unused
   B. have the item inspected or tested and then have the supplier advised of the results
   C. retain it in the purchasing department
   D. purchase a quantity of the product

10. The one of the following factors which is NOT pertinent to consider in determining whether a bidder is responsible is the bidder's

    A. financial resources
    B. technical resources
    C. reputation among other buyers
    D. reputation among other suppliers

11. When may a sealed bid be changed by a potential supplier?

    A. Never
    B. Any time before the closing date
    C. After the closing date but before the bids are opened
    D. After the bids are opened but before an award is made

12. When a buyer asks for a quotation on an item that is specified in detail, he may accept a substitute ONLY if

    A. the item as specified is not manufactured in this country
    B. the item as specified is out of stock in the successful bidder's warehouse
    C. there is substantial compliance with the item as specified
    D. there was only one vendor who could supply the item as specified

13. The one of the following which should NOT be considered by a buyer when determining the low bid is the

    A. discount from list price B. f.o.b. terms
    C. advertised retail price D. cash discount

14. In purchasing, the specification for a technical commodity which is to be purchased should be developed by the

    A. buyer alone
    B. buyer and the agency involved
    C. salesman for a potential supplier
    D. research department of a potential supplier

15. During a period of rising prices, which one of the following options would be MOST advisable for a buyer to select?

    A. *Price at the time of delivery* contracts
    B. *Hand to mouth* purchases
    C. Long term *fixed price* contracts
    D. *Spot* contracts

16. A standardization program is BEST established and has the MOST opportunity of succeeding if it is developed

    A. by representatives from successful suppliers in past years
    B. by the senior purchasing officers
    C. and approved by a committee of representatives from city agencies and the purchasing department
    D. by a citizens' committee

17. A purchase order that has been acknowledged and accepted by the vendor may be cancelled by the city if the

    A. city agency involved has no available funds in its budget
    B. buyer finds a cheaper substitute
    C. vendor agrees to accept a cancellation
    D. vendor submits an invoice before shipping the order

18. Assume that you have received four identical bids for a large quantity of a brand name item and it has been agreed that there is no good substitute for it.
    In this situation, you SHOULD recommend that the award be made to the supplier

    A. who sold the item to the city the last time it was purchased
    B. who originally brought the item to your attention
    C. who regularly advertises the product on television
    D. whose warehouse and office are located within the city limits

19. Suppose that a buyer establishes the mode and routing of transportation of a purchased commodity.
The one of the following which is NOT a valid reason for doing so is to insure that the shipment arrives

    A. in top condition
    B. in returnable containers
    C. at the most economical cost
    D. on schedule

    19.____

20. Suppose that a buyer has been asked to outfit a small room in an agency's building as a library. He asks Supplier X, who manufactures library equipment and has an architect on his staff, to develop a plan and suggest equipment for the room. Supplier X submits blueprints, equipment lists, and an installed price of $50,000. The agency is delighted with the proposed plan and approves it. It would then be MOST appropriate for the buyer to

    A. award the order to Supplier X
    B. pay Supplier X for the plans only and then ask Suppliers X, Y, and Z to bid on these plans
    C. ask Suppliers Y and Z to develop plans, then award the order to the low bidder of the three
    D. use Supplier X's plans and lists, ask Suppliers Y and Z to submit prices, and then award to the low bidder

    20.____

KEY (CORRECT ANSWERS)

1.	A	11.	B
2.	D	12.	C
3.	A	13.	C
4.	D	14.	B
5.	D	15.	C
6.	C	16.	C
7.	A	17.	C
8.	D	18.	D
9.	B	19.	B
10.	D	20.	B

TEST 2

DIRECTIONS: Each question or incomplete statement is followed by several suggested answers or completions. Select the one that BEST answers the question or completes the statement. *PRINT THE LETTER OF THE CORRECT ANSWER IN THE SPACE AT THE RIGHT.*

1. Purchasing the proper quantity is a responsibility of a buyer.
   Buying small quantities at a time is likely to result in a reduction in the number of

   A. purchasing personnel
   B. purchase orders issued
   C. quantity price discounts received
   D. invoices to be paid

   1._____

2. Of the following factors, the one that should NOT be considered by a buyer when determining the quantity of an item to be ordered is the

   A. quantity price differentials
   B. cash discount terms offered
   C. rate of past use
   D. shelf life or possible deterioration if kept in inventory too long

   2._____

3. A buyer may make a purchase WITHOUT negotiation when

   A. the commodity has been purchased previously without negotiation
   B. the commodity costs relatively little in dollars and cents
   C. a requirement contract has been established for the commodity
   D. a brand name is required

   3._____

4. The one of the following which is the proper quality guide for a commodity to be purchased that will give the BEST value for the money expended is the

   A. quality suitable for the intended use
   B. best quality of the item
   C. cheapest quality available
   D. best quality manufactured locally

   4._____

5. Which one of the following would NOT constitute proper use of a buyer's association with a salesman?

   A. Develop interest in all the salesman's products among city agencies
   B. Accelerate delivery of the salesman's firm's product to meet a deadline
   C. Acquaint the buyer with the method by which the salesman's firm manufactures its product
   D. Acquaint the buyer with other products produced by the salesman's firm

   5._____

6. A supplier's catalog is GENERALLY regarded by a buyer or purchasing agent as a publication that

   A. lists the prices at which the products shown must be sold
   B. invites business with the firm for the products illustrated
   C. assures that the composition of the products will be maintained as described
   D. assures that the products illustrated are carried in stock

   6._____

25

7. One of the duties of a buyer is to maintain up-to-date mailing lists of prospective bidders. The BEST reason for maintaining such lists is that they

   A. make it unnecessary for the buyer to formally advertise for bids
   B. provide a convenient and accurate record of sources of supply
   C. enable a buyer to identify and eliminate vendors who have been consistently high bidders in the past
   D. provide a group of vendors who are sure to submit bids

8. Suppose that a city agency needs 20 one-gallon cans of cleaner. Which of the following MOST adequately describes the quantity needed? _____ cleaner

   A. 20 gallons
   B. 80 quarts
   C. 4 five-gallon cans
   D. 20 x 1 gallon cans of

9. *Expediting delivery* means

   A. assisting in unloading a shipment
   B. making certain that the supplier knows where to send the material
   C. offering containers in which the goods may be shipped
   D. taking action to assure delivery of goods purchased in accordance with a time schedule

10. Once a purchase order has been sent to the vendor, a buyer is NOT relieved of further responsibility until he has been notified that the

    A. agency wanted a different color of the item
    B. item was accepted
    C. time delivered did not meet specifications
    D. item was damaged on arrival

11. Which one of the following is the MOST important reason for stocking a commodity in a central storehouse?

    A. A local supplier can deliver about as quickly as the central storehouse.
    B. City agencies have not standardized the commodity.
    C. The commodity is used by the city agencies all during the year.
    D. Some city agencies lack space for storing the commodity.

12. Which one of the following describes a *seller's market*?

    A. Demand exceeds supply
    B. Supply exceeds demand
    C. Goods are easy to purchase
    D. The buyer demands and gets his price for the goods

13. The one of the following bonds which is NOT generally used in city purchasing is a _____ bond.

    A. surety
    B. performance
    C. bid
    D. payment

14. A buyer is MOST likely to obtain commodities of the proper quality at the right price if he

    A. consistently awards purchase orders to the lowest bidder
    B. carefully prepares specifications for required commodities
    C. accepts bids only from large suppliers
    D. purchases brand name commodities whenever possible

15. The term *f.o.b.* is a

    A. shipping term
    B. trade discount term
    C. cash payment demand
    D. quality term

16. Traffic, a purchasing responsibility, is defined as the

    A. method of delivery and routing of commodities ordered
    B. packaging of commodities ordered
    C. time of delivery of commodities ordered
    D. quantity of items to be delivered

17. A back order is a(n)

    A. order that is more than 90 days behind the scheduled delivery
    B. portion of an order the vendor cannot deliver at the scheduled time and has reentered for future delivery
    C. order that is repeated in identically the same terms as a previous order
    D. portion of an order that has been recalled and cancelled

18. The term *f.o.b. destination* signifies that it is the

    A. buyer's obligation and expense to get the goods from the seller's factory
    B. seller's obligation and expense to deliver the goods to the buyer
    C. seller's obligation to deliver the goods to the buyer at the buyer's expense
    D. buyer's duty to insure the merchandise against loss

19. When an *escalator clause* is used, it would ordinarily be found in a _____ contract.

    A. *fixed price*
    B. *spot*
    C. *price at the time of delivery*
    D. *cost plus*

20. In purchasing, lead time is GENERALLY considered to be the period of time from the date of

    A. order to date of delivery
    B. requisition to date of delivery
    C. quotation request to date of delivery
    D. requisition to date of order

KEY (CORRECT ANSWERS)

1.	C	11.	C
2.	B	12.	A
3.	B	13.	A
4.	A	14.	B
5.	A	15.	A
6.	B	16.	A
7.	B	17.	B
8.	D	18.	B
9.	D	19.	C
10.	B	20.	B

EXAMINATION SECTION
TEST 1

DIRECTIONS: Each question or incomplete statement is followed by several suggested answers or completions. Select the one that BEST answers the question or completes the statement. *PRINT THE LETTER OF THE CORRECT ANSWER IN THE SPACE AT THE RIGHT.*

1. The purchase of goods *as is* includes a(n)   1.____

   A. warranty
   B. guarantee
   C. assurance of the condition of the goods
   D. assurance of the quantity available

2. A change order becomes legally binding after approval by the   2.____

   A. agency involved and the buyer
   B. buyer alone
   C. vendor alone
   D. chief purchasing officer and the vendor

3. Of the following courses of action, the MOST advisable one for a buyer to take in order to obtain an item costing under $100 in the shortest time possible would be to   3.____

   A. call in several vendors with whom he has dealt previously and discuss price and availability of the item
   B. invite all vendors who carry the item to submit written bids
   C. consult the classified telephone directory to find a local vendor and purchase the item directly
   D. try to locate the item in another agency's storehouse

4. A buyer SHOULD begin his analysis of bids by   4.____

   A. tabulating the bids received
   B. checking on the responsibility of all the bidders
   C. selecting the apparently high bids for consideration
   D. eliminating the bids from suppliers who have been consistently high bidders in the past

5. A buyer should make a recommendation for the award of a contract to the supplier who offers the   5.____

   A. lowest price
   B. suitable quality
   C. suitable quality and lowest price
   D. best value

6. Before recommending that a low bidder be awarded a contract for a certain commodity, a buyer SHOULD   6.____

A. ask other buyers what they consider a reasonable price for that commodity
B. check the low bidder's price against price indices to make sure that it is reasonable
C. make sure that he does not recommend accepting a bid at a higher price than that which was paid the last time the item was purchased
D. tell the bidder that he has a better chance of winning the contract if he will lower his price

7. When purchases are made by brand name, it USUALLY follows that the

   A. buyer does not has to be concerned with the quality of the commodity
   B. brand name commodity is superior in quality to other materials in the field
   C. buyer depends upon the integrity and reliability of the company that produces the commodity
   D. buyer is not required to advertise for bids on the commodity

8. Assume that a buyer asks for informal written quotations for a certain quantity of a commodity from four suppliers. He receives almost identical bids. He suspects collusion. In this situation, it would be MOST advisable for the buyer to

   A. attempt to get four additional suppliers to bid
   B. draw lots to determine the successful bidder
   C. ask each supplier to rebid on the same specifications
   D. reject all bids, revise specifications, and advertise for new bids

9. Of the following, the MOST important reason for a buyer to place contracts or purchase orders only with responsible bidders is that

   A. the buyer may be blamed if a bidder defaults
   B. irresponsible bidders usually charge high prices
   C. if a bidder defaults, the agency involved may be without supplies during the time it takes to accept new bids
   D. a responsible bidder always supplies goods of superior quality

10. Suppose that sealed bids are received from four suppliers. Supplier A bid $1 per unit; the next lowest bid was $1.12 per unit. The award is made to Supplier A. After receiving the contract, Supplier A tells the buyer that he made a mistake in his price and it should have been 10% higher.
    In this situation, it would be BEST for the buyer to

    A. rebid the entire requirement
    B. agree to pay $1.10 per unit to Supplier A
    C. disqualify Supplier A and award the contract to the supplier who bid $1.12 per unit
    D. insist that Supplier A fill the order at $1 per unit or recommend that the order be cancelled and charge him the cost of obtaining the goods elsewhere

11. *Or equal* bidding requires that awards be

    A. made only on the basis of samples submitted by the bidder
    B. based upon comparative prices
    C. made only where essential characteristics of the goods comply with specifications advertised
    D. made only after bids from at least three regular suppliers have been considered and rejected

12. Suppose that a salesman sends a buyer tickets for six box seats at a World Series baseball game.
    In this situation, it would be MOST advisable for the buyer to

    A. divide the tickets among the purchasing department personnel
    B. donate the tickets to a charitable institution
    C. return the tickets to the salesman
    D. use the tickets to entertain visiting purchasing personnel

13. Which one of the following actions is ordinarily considered ACCEPTABLE purchasing practice?

    A. Asking for quotations from six suppliers and then deciding not to order any of the commodity
    B. Taking a cash discount of 2%, offered under 2/10 net 30, thirty days after receipt of the invoice and the material
    C. Requesting a quotation for 2,000 lbs. of paper and then ordering 125 lbs. at the 2,000 lb. price
    D. Asking a supplier for a sample of an item to fill an agency's need for only one of the items

14. Suppose that a purchase order for $50,000 of steel is placed, specifying delivery via barge. The price quoted includes cost of delivery and the terms are 2% 10 days. The invoice is dated April 1, and it arrives on April 3. A bill of lading for the shipment is dated April 4, and the steel arrives May 20.
    The 2% cash discount may be taken if the invoice is paid within 10 days after

    A. May 20   B. April 4   C. April 3   D. April 1

15. The term *caveat emptor* means:

    A. Let the seller beware
    B. The seller guarantees the quality
    C. Let the buyer beware
    D. Let the seller warrant the item

16. Which one of the following is NOT conducive to good communications between city purchasing personnel and suppliers?
    A

    A. friendly manner   B. firm but courteous manner
    C. personal approach   D. curt and brisk manner

17. You may, on occasion, interview vendors who wish to be placed on the bidder's list. When conducting such an interview, it would generally be considered MOST appropriate for you to

    A. imply that the vendor is likely to receive a number of contract awards if he submits a lot of bids
    B. stress that the vendor will have a lot of competition
    C. explain the bid process and answer the vendor's questions
    D. try to determine whether the vendor will actually submit any bids

18. Suppose that a buyer receives a request from a vendor for information which the buyer knows is confidential.
In this situation, it would usually be MOST desirable for the buyer to

    A. tell the vendor that the information he is asking for is confidential
    B. give the vendor the information in order to maintain friendly relations with him
    C. rebuke the vendor for asking for confidential information
    D. tell the vendor to call the supervising buyer in order to obtain the information

19. Suppose that a vendor who has bid for the first time is not awarded the contract. He calls you to complain, claiming that he offered exactly what the bid proposal specified.
In this situation, it would usually be MOST desirable for you to tell this vendor

    A. that all bids are carefully analyzed, and if he had deserved the award, he would have gotten it
    B. that if he is not satisfied with the decision he need not submit any bids in the future
    C. to submit other bids in the future, and he will surely be successful
    D. how bids are analyzed and why his bid was rejected

20. Suppose that you have been working as a buyer for a short time. You have a question regarding a purchase transaction you are handling, and, because your supervisor is not available at the time, you ask a fellow buyer how to proceed. The procedure he tells you to follow seems contrary to previous instructions you have received.
In this situation, the one of the following courses of action it would usually be BEST for you to follow would be to

    A. tell your fellow worker that he is giving you incorrect information
    B. thank your fellow worker for his assistance and wait for your supervisor to be available before proceeding
    C. ask your fellow worker if he will handle the purchase transaction for you
    D. follow the procedure your fellow worker told you and if it proves to be incorrect, explain to your supervisor that you were given wrong information by your fellow worker

KEY (CORRECT ANSWERS)

1. D
2. D
3. C
4. A
5. C

6. B
7. C
8. D
9. C
10. D

11. C
12. C
13. A
14. D
15. C

16. D
17. C
18. A
19. D
20. B

TEST 2

DIRECTIONS: Each question or incomplete statement is followed by several suggested answers or completions. Select the one that BEST answers the question or completes the statement. *PRINT THE LETTER OF THE CORRECT ANSWER IN THE SPACE AT THE RIGHT.*

1. Suppose that you purchase 100 units of an item at a list of $1 per unit less 40% and 10%, and less 2% if paid within 10 days.
   If payment is made within the ten-day limit, the amount of the payment would be

   A. $52.92   B. $54.00   C. $58.80   D. $60.00

   1._____

2. Another way of saying 1 3/4 gross is

   A. 144 individual units   B. 7 dozen
   C. 21 dozen   D. 250 individual units

   2._____

3. Assume that a buyer had to purchase 40,000 lbs. of salt. Which one of the following bids SHOULD he accept, assuming quality, service, and delivery terms are all the same?

   A. 1¢ per pound, 2%-30 days
   B. 99¢ per 100 lbs., 1%-30 days
   C. $19 per ton, 1%-30 days
   D. $18 per ton, net-30 days

   3._____

4. Which one of the following four bids represents the BEST value, assuming delivery costs amount to $100?

   A. $1000 f.o.b. buyer, less 2%-10 days
   B. $900 f.o.b. seller, less 2%-10 days
   C. $975 delivered, net cash 30 days
   D. $990 f.o.b. buyer, less 1 %-10 days

   4._____

5. Suppose that four suppliers make the following offers to sell 2,000 units of a particular commodity.
   Which one is the MOST advantageous proposal?

   A. $10 list, less 40% and 5%
   B. $5 cost, plus 20% to cover overhead and profit
   C. $10 list, less 20% and 20%
   D. $5 cost, plus 10% overhead and 10% for profit

   5._____

Questions 6-7.

DIRECTIONS: Answer Questions 6 and 7 SOLELY on the basis of the information contained in the following chart, which plots the average price of a commodity during the calendar years indicated.

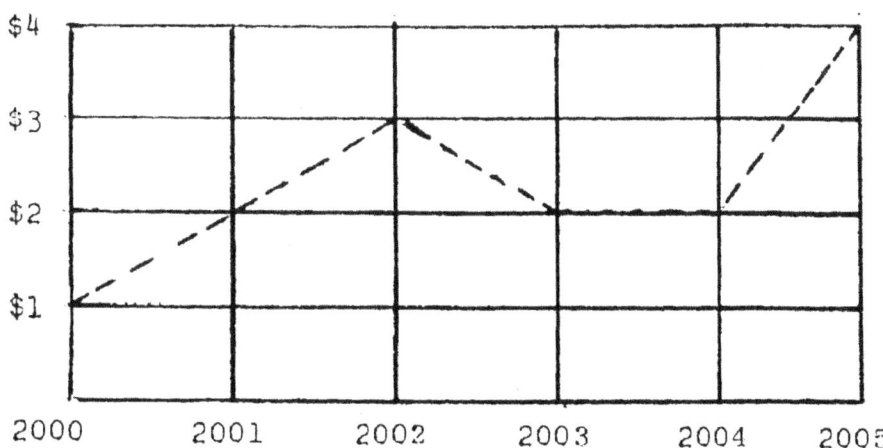

6. According to the above chart, the increase in the average price of the commodity from 2002 to 2005 was APPROXIMATELY   6._____

   A. 25%   B. 33 1/3%   C. 50%   D. 75%

7. According to the above chart, the increase in the average price of the commodity from 2000 to 2002 was APPROXIMATELY   7._____

   A. 20%   B. 30%   C. 200%   D. 300%

Questions 8-9.

DIRECTIONS: Answer Questions 8 and 9 SOLELY on the basis of the information contained in the chart below, which shows supply and demand of a commodity from January 1, 2001 to January 1, 2005.

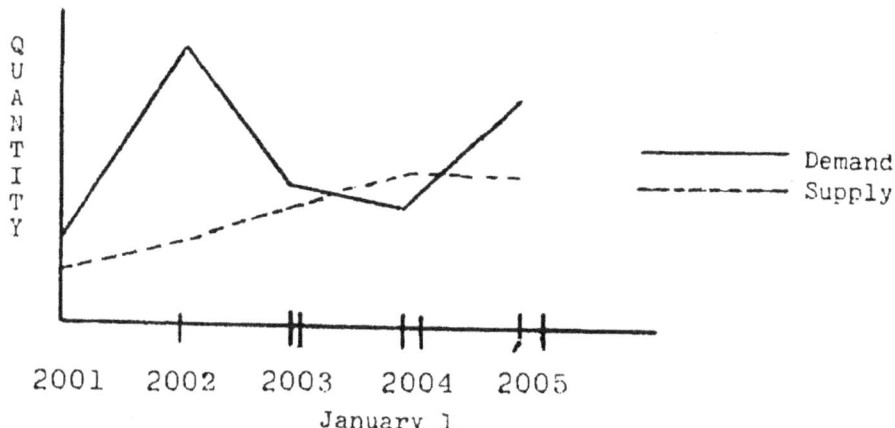

8. The above chart indicates that there was a seller's market during most of each of the following years EXCEPT   8._____

   A. 2001   B. 2002   C. 2003   D. 2004

9. According to the above chart, in the absence of price controls or other artificial or unusual circumstances, when would the price of the commodity have been the HIGHEST?
   January 1,

   A. 2001   B. 2002   C. 2003   D. 2004

10. Assume that the 1967 cost of living factor was 100 and that a certain product was selling that year for $5 per unit. Assume further that at the present time, the cost of living factor is 150.
    If the selling price of the product increased 10% more than the cost of living during this period, at the present time, the product would be selling for____ per unit.

    A. $8.25   B. $10.50   C. $16.50   D. $7.75

Questions 11-15.

DIRECTIONS: Questions 11 through 15 are to be answered on the basis of the instructions and paragraph which follow.

Instructions for answering Questions 11 through 15: The paragraph which follows is part of a report prepared by a buyer for submission to his superior.

The paragraph contains 5 underlined groups of words, each one bearing a number which identifies the question relating to it. Each of these groups of words MAY or MAY NOT represent correct written standard English suitable for use in a formal report. For each question, decide whether the group of words used in the paragraph which is always choice A, is correct written standard English and should be retained, or whether choice B, C, or D. Print the letter of the correct answer in the space at the right.

On October 23, 2005 the vendor delivered to microscopes to the using agency.

When they inspected, one microscope was found to have a defective part. The vendor
            11
was notified, and offered to replace the defective part; the using agency, however,

requested that the microscope be replaced. The vendor claimed that complete
                    12
replacement was unnecessary and refused to comply with the agency's demand,

having the result that the agency declared that it will pay only for the acceptable
                13
microscope. At that point I got involved by the agency's contacting me. The agency
                                        14
requested that I speak to the vendor since I handled the original purchase and

have dealed with this vendor before.
            15

11. A. When they inspected,
    B. Upon inspection,
    C. The inspection report said that
    D. Having inspected,

11.____

12. A. that the microscope be replaced.
    B. a whole new microscope in replacement.
    C. to have a replacement for the microscope.
    D. that they get the microscope replaced.

12.____

13. A. , having the result that the agency declared
    B. ; the agency consequently declared
    C. , which refusal caused the agency to consequently declare
    D. , with the result of the agency's declaring

13.____

14. A. I got involved by the agency's contacting me.
    B. I became involved, being contacted by the agency.
    C. the agency contacting me, I got involved,
    D. the agency contacted me and I became involved.

14.____

15. A. have dealed with this vendor before.
    B. done business before with this vendor.
    C. know this vendor by prior dealings.
    D. have dealt with this vendor before.

15.____

Questions 16-18.

DIRECTIONS: Answer Questions 16 through 18 on the basis of the following letter, which was prepared by a buyer in response to a letter of inquiry from a prospective bidder.

Mr. Fred Stewart
XYZ Manufacturing Company
200 West Street
Chicago, Illinois 21783

Dear Mr. Stewart:

    To answer your question – yes, sometimes the City buys things from out-of-town people. If you're really interested in bidding, the Office of Vendor Relations can send you some forms to fill out. Then you can get on the bidders list and you won't miss any chances to bid because we'll notify you automatically. You could just submit a bid, but before you could be awarded a contract you would have to fill out the forms anyway.

    Hope this information answers your question.

                                            Very truly yours,
                                            John Jones

16. Which one of the following criticisms of the style in which the above letter is written is MOST appropriate?
    The

    A. A. language is ambiguous
    B. letter Hacks concreteness
    C. language is too colloquial
    D. letter is too brief

17. The impression that the recipient is MOST likely to get from the above letter is

    A. *favorable,* because the tone of the letter is friendly
    B. *unfavorable,* because of the unprofessional tone of the letter
    C. *favorable,* because the letter is encouraging
    D. *unfavorable,* because the letter is not sufficiently courteous

18. Of the following changes suggested to the buyer, which one would have MOST improved the above letter?

    A. Refer specifically to the recipient's original letter of inquiry
    B. Give all the infornmtion necessary for the recipient to take appropriate action
    C. Offer to send the recipient some informative literature
    D. Directly encourage the recipient to do business with the City

Questions 19-20.

DIRECTIONS: Base your answers to Questions 19 and 20 on the following passage.

The City Charter requires that all purchases be made according to definite standards, or specifications. A specification may be defined as a statement of particulars descriptive of materials, or performance, or both; or, as a description of the technical details of a required commodity or service; or as a statement of what the buyer wants the seller to furnish. The specification should concisely define the quality of the commodity that is required to meet the needs of the using agency but still provide as wide competition in sources of supply as possible. To be of maximum value, the specification should describe the commodity clearly and in sufficient detail to ensure obtaining the exact commodity required.

19. Suppose that a buyer prepared the following specification for an item: cotton, absorbent, rolled.
    Based on the information given in the above passage, this specification would NOT be of value MAINLY because the

    A. quality of cotton required is not described
    B. description is not concise
    C. mode of packaging is not stated
    D. using agency is not referred to

20. Based on the information given in the above passage, the MOST important indication that a specification has been well prepared is that the

    A. buyer gets few bids on the commodity
    B. commodity obtained meets the needs of the using agency
    C. commodity is procured at the lowest possible cost
    D. commodity is described in great detail

20.____

KEY (CORRECT ANSWERS)

1.	A	11.	B
2.	C	12.	A
3.	D	13.	B
4.	C	14.	D
5.	A	15.	D
6.	B	16.	C
7.	C	17.	B
8.	C	18.	B
9.	B	19.	A
10.	A	20.	B

EXAMINATION SECTION
TEST 1

DIRECTIONS: Each question or incomplete statement is followed by several suggested answers or completions. Select the one that BEST answers the question or completes the statement. *PRINT THE LETTER OF THE CORRECT ANSWER IN THE SPACE AT THE RIGHT.*

1. Which one of the following is NOT an advantage of centralized purchasing?

    A. Preferential discounts can be secured for quantity contracts.
    B. Higher yields are obtained from disposal of excess surplus, scrap, and salvage.
    C. Savings from elimination of duplicated personnel are effected.
    D. Purchases are made more directly and promptly.

    1.____

2. Of the following, the record that has the LEAST relevancy to the purchasing procedure is the

    A. commodity purchase record
    B. purchase requisition
    C. request for quotation
    D. stores requisition

    2.____

3. While quantity purchases generally represent a saving over smaller purchases, an astute buyer realizes that many facts must be considered before seeking price reduction through quantity alone.
Of the chief factors to be considered, the one which is of LEAST importance is

    A. obsolescence
    B. handling and distribution
    C. price analysis
    D. possible deterioration

    3.____

4. The one of the following factors which should be LEAST considered when selecting a bid is

    A. responsibility of the bidder
    B. price, discounts, and quality of material offered
    C. capacity of the bidder to engage in reciprocity
    D. delivery date

    4.____

5. If you are considering the names *IBM* and *Smith-Corona* as possible sources of supply for a certain item, the one of the following which you would MOST probably add to the list is

    A. Admiral   B. 3M   C. Toshiba   D. Olivetti

    5.____

6. Which one of the following is it LEAST important to consider when selecting the right vendor?

    A. Maintenance costs of a higher bidder are significantly lower than that of the lowest bidder.
    B. The vendor has a tax hearing pending with the Federal government.
    C. The vendor has frequent strikes in his plant.
    D. The vendor is often late in making deliveries.

    6.____

7. After a vendor deposits his bid with the purchasing department, when if at all, may it be withdrawn by him?

   A. At any time
   B. Before the award is made
   C. It may not be withdrawn
   D. Prior to the opening

8. The one of the following which is NOT a publication of value to buyers and purchasing agents is

   A. DUN'S REVIEW
   B. FORBES
   C. FORTUNE
   D. MILL AND FACTORY

9. Which one of the following is NOT a credit reporting agency?

   A. Allen Reports, Inc.
   B. Dun and Bradstreet
   C. Harcourt-Brace
   D. Skip-Tracers, Inc.

10. Of the following, the reference item which is NOT of value in assisting the buyer to determine whether a price bid is fair and reasonable is

    A. commodity journals
    B. price experience
    C. price indices
    D. Sweet's catalogs

11. The term *sellers' market* refers to a condition where

    A. costs of procurement are high but costs of expediting will be insubstantial
    B. economic waste is discouraged
    C. supply is less than demand
    D. there is an overabundance of the materials involved

12. Use of the expression in sales agreement that goods are sold *as is* implies that

    A. buyer will have recourse on the vendor for the quality of the goods but not for the condition
    B. buyer is taking delivery of goods in some way defective
    C. goods offered may be damaged but must be in substantially workable condition
    D. the usual warranty will apply to the transaction if the vendor is guilty of concealment

13. A contract in which buyer and seller both understand that the goods which are exhibited constitute the standard with which the goods not exhibited correspond, and to which deliveries should conform, is known as a sale

    A. by sample
    B. with right of redemption
    C. by consignment
    D. of fungibles

14. The one of the following that is NOT a specification and code-making organization is American _____ Association.

    A. Gas
    B. Management
    C. Standards
    D. Water Works

15. Assume that bids are received for certain castings. The specification on which the bids are based states that a tolerance of 1/32 inch on a certain dimension will be permitted. The buyer knows that actually the castings will be accepted if they are within 1/16 of an inch of the tolerance limit. A prospective bidder on these castings contacts the buyer and asks whether the 1/32 inch tolerance must be adhered to. The buyer informs him that in all probability the castings will be accepted if they are within 1/16 of an inch of the tolerance limit. Such action by the buyer is generally 15.____

    A. *ethical* provided he refuses any gifts or favors from the bidder
    B. *ethical* provided the buyer is certain he knows the permitted tolerance limit exactly
    C. *unethical* since the bidder is at a competitive advantage
    D. *unethical* since the buyer has placed himself under an obligation to the bidder

16. *Contract date* is the date 16.____

    A. the contract is prepared or typed
    B. the contract is acknowledged by the seller
    C. the buyer returns the contract to the seller
    D. when the contract is accepted by all parties thereto

17. When a buyer wittingly solicits a favored price, discriminatory to other competing customers, he may be in violation of the 17.____

    A. Clayton Act, as amended   B. Food, Drug, and Cosmetic Act
    C. Federal Trade Commission Act   D. Sherman Anti-Trust Act

18. Of the following elements, which is LEAST necessary in order for a contract to be valid and binding? 18.____

    A. Competent parties   B. Consideration
    C. Legality of subject matter   D. Written acceptance

19. A *standard package discount* refers to the discount allowed 19.____

    A. according to the number of packages purchased
    B. if the purchaser agreed to buy the vendor's regular package
    C. on the package content determined by the buyer
    D. when more than one of an item is purchased

20. Which one of the following defines the term *cost-plus* best?
The 20.____

    A. cost to produce the item plus a stated percentage of fixed sum
    B. cost to produce the item plus packing costs
    C. cost to produce the item plus shipping costs
    D. original cost of the item to the buyer plus all costs involved until it is ultimately used

21. When an item is shipped on *consignment*, 21.____

    A. the item becomes part of the buyer's inventory
    B. the purchaser must pay for the item upon receipt
    C. title in the item remains with the seller
    D. title passes to the buyer upon receipt of the item

22. The term *escalation* means which one of the following? A provision

    A. allowing for an increase in a contract price based on pre-determined contingencies
    B. for increasing the rate of payments due under a purchase contract
    C. for increasing the rate of production on a purchase requirement resulting in earlier deliveries
    D. for requiring earlier than contracted for deliveries

23. Of the following, the term *liquidated damages* is BEST defined as

    A. a sum agreed upon between the buyer and seller to be paid by the party who breaches the contract
    B. a varying amount which is to be paid by the seller to the buyer if the commodity is seized or destroyed by governmental authority
    C. the costs assessed when a liquid commodity is damaged during return shipment to the manufacturer
    D. the costs assessed when a liquid commodity is damaged prior to receipt by the purchaser

24. When used in the field of transportation, the term *prepaid* means MOST NEARLY the

    A. purchaser agrees to pay all costs involved in the purchase, including the cost of the service or item plus transportation costs, prior to shipment being made
    B. purchaser has agreed to pay all transportation charges involved in the purchase prior to receipt of the goods
    C. seller has agreed to pay all return transportation charges if the buyer later decides not to accept the goods
    D. seller has agreed to pay all transportation charges involved in the purchase

25. Which of the following statements is FALSE?

    A. Brass is an alloy of copper and zinc.
    B. Bronze is an alloy of copper and tin.
    C. Mild steel is also known as low carbon steel.
    D. Stainless steel pipe type 304 weighs about the same as steel pipe given the same thickness and length.

26. With respect to purchases of glass, *Type I* refers to

    A. price
    B. resistance to breakage
    C. resistance to high temperatures and chemicals
    D. size

27. Paper is *calendared* to

    A. impress the logotype of the mill on it
    B. make it smooth
    C. permit successive pages to be consecutively numbered
    D. record the date of its manufacture

28. The term *prime contractor* refers to the 28.____

    A. firm with which the city has entered into a direct contract for supplies and materials
    B. firm that undertakes to perform a job but which releases control of the means and manner of accomplishing the desired result
    C. first vendor to submit a price
    D. vendor who manufactures against a sub-contract

29. A manufacturer's agent 29.____

    A. cannot spread costs over a number of lines
    B. represents the purchaser
    C. serves as a manufacturer's sales organization
    D. takes title to merchandise he sells

30. The abbreviation LCL is MOST closely associated with which one of the following modes of transportation? 30.____

    A. Air   B. Rail   C. Ship   D. Truck

31. The term *2 percent E.O.M. - 10* means that 31.____

    A. if an error or omission is reported by the buyer within 10 days of receipt of a shipment, a 2 percent discount is allowed
    B. a 2 percent discount is allowed if payment is made on or before the 10th of the following month
    C. a 2 percent discount is allowed if payment is made on or before the 10th day of the month in which shipment is made whether or not the shipment has been received
    D. a 2 percent discount is allowed if the invoice is paid within 10 days of its receipt

32. In a *conditional* sale, 32.____

    A. possession only of the item is retained by the seller
    B. the title and possession is retained by the seller
    C. the title and possession passes to the purchaser
    D. the title only is retained by the seller

33. Which one of the following is NOT a method of specification? Specification by 33.____

    A. chemical analysis   B. custom
    C. physical description   D. sample

Questions 34-36.

DIRECTIONS: Questions 34 through 36 are to be answered on the basis of the following passage.

The State Assembly has passed a bill that would require all state agencies, public authoritites, and local governments to refuse bids in excess of $2,000 from any foreign firm or corporation. The only exceptions to this outright prohibition against public buying of foreign goods or services would be for products not available in this country, goods of a quality unobtainable from an American supplier, and products using foreign materials that are *substantially* manufactured in the United States.

The bill is a flagrant violation of the United States' officially espoused trade principles. It would add to the costs of state and local governments. It could provoke retaliatory action from many foreign governments against the state and other American producers, and foreign governments would be fully entitled to take such retaliatory action under the General Agreement on Tariffs and Trade, which the United States has signed.

The State Senate, which now has the Assembly bill before it, should reject this protectionist legislation out of enlightened regard for the interests of the taxpayers and producers of the state — as well as for those of the nation and its trading partners generally. In this time of unemployment and international monetary disorder, the state — with its reputation for intelligent and progressive law-making — should avoid contributing to what could become a tidal wave of protectionism here and overseas.

34. Under the requirements of the bill passed by the State Assembly, a bid from a foreign manufacturer in excess of $2,000 can be accepted by a state agency or local government only if it meets which one of the following requirements?
The

    A. bid is approved individually by the state legislature
    B. bidder is willing to accept payment in United States currency
    C. bid is for an item of a quality unobtainable from an American supplier
    D. bid is for an item which would be more expensive if it were purchased from an American supplier

35. The author of the above passage feels that the bill passed by the State Assembly should be

    A. passed by the State Senate and put into effect
    B. passed by the State Senate but vetoed by the Governor
    C. reintroduced into the State Assembly and rejected
    D. rejected by the State Senate

36. The author of the passage calls the practice of prohibiting purchase of products manufactured by foreign countries

    A. prohibition   B. protectionism
    C. retaliatory action   D. isolationism

37. Of the following, the one that defines *buyer's option* best is:
The

    A. buyer may purchase the item or items at his convenience
    B. buyer must effectuate the purchase sooner or later
    C. price, time, and conditions are usually agreed upon in advance
    D. price to be paid will be determined at the time the option is exercised

38. Proprietary article is a(n)

    A. article manufactured and sold by a patentee
    B. franchised item
    C. individual piece or thing of a class
    D. medicinal compound

7 (#1)

39. Assume that it is necessary to partition a room measuring 40 feet by 20 feet into eight smaller rooms of equal size. Allowing no room for aisles, the MINIMUM amount of partitioning that would be needed is _____ feet.

    A. 90   B. 100   C. 110   D. 140

40. Assume that two types of files have been ordered: 200 of type A and 100 of type B. When the files are delivered, the buyer discovers that 25% of each type is damaged. Of the remaining files, 20% of type A and 40% of type B are the wrong color. The total number of files that are the WRONG color is

    A. 30   B. 40   C. 50   D. 60

Questions 41-50.

DIRECTIONS: Questions 41 through 50 are to be answered solely on the basis of the following table showing the amounts purchased by various purchasing units during 2007.

DOLLAR VOLUME PURCHASED BY EACH PURCHASING UNIT DURING EACH QUARTER OF 2007
(FIGURES SHOWN REPRESENT THOUSANDS OF DOLLARS)

Purchasing Unit	First Quarter	Second Quarter	Third Quarter	Fourth Quarter
A	578	924	698	312
B	1,426	1,972	1,586	1,704
C	366	494	430	716
D	1,238	1,708	1,884	1,546
E	730	742	818	774
F	948	1,118	1,256	788

41. The total dollar volume purchased by all of the purchasing units during 2007 approximated MOST NEARLY

    A. $2,000,000   B. $4,000,000
    C. $20,000,000   D. $40,000,000

42. During which quarter was the GREATEST total dollar amount of purchases made?

    A. First   B. Second   C. Third   D. Fourth

43. Assume that the dollar volume purchased by Unit F during 2007 exceeded the dollar volume purchased by Unit F during 2006 by 50%.
Then, the dollar volume purchased by Unit F during 2006 was

    A. $2,055,000   B. $2,550,000
    C. $2,740,000   D. $6,165,000

8 (#1)

44. Which one of the following purchasing units showed the sharpest DECREASE in the amount purchased during the fourth quarter as compared with the third quarter?
Unit

   A. A   B. B   C. D   D. E

44.____

45. Comparing the dollar volume purchased in the second quarter with the dollar volume purchased in the third quarter, the decrease in the dollar volume during the third quarter was PRIMARILY due to the decrease in the dollar volume purchased by Units _____ and _____.

   A. A; B   B. C; D   C. C; E   D. C; F

45.____

46. Of the following, the unit which had the LARGEST number of dollars of increased purchases from any one quarter to the next following quarter was Unit

   A. A   B. B   C. C   D. D

46.____

47. Of the following, the unit with the LARGEST dollar volume of purchases during the second half of 2007 was Unit

   A. A   B. B   C. D   D. F

47.____

48. Which one of the following MOST closely approximates the percentage which Unit B's total 2007 purchases represents of the total 2007 purchases of all units, including Unit B?

   A. 10%   B. 15%   C. 25%   D. 45%

48.____

49. Assume that research showed that each ten thousand dollars ($10,000) of purchases by Unit D during 2007 required an average of thirteen (13) man-hours of buyers' staff time. On that basis, which one of the following MOST closely approximates the number of man-hours of buyers' staff time required by Unit D during 2007?
_____ man-hours.

   A. 1,800   B. 8,000   C. 68,000   D. 78,000

49.____

50. Assume that research showed that each ten thousand dollars ($10,000) of purchases by Unit C during 2007 required an average of ten (10) man-hours of buyers' staff time. This research also showed that during 2007 the average man-hours of buyers' staff time per ten thousand dollars of purchases required by Unit C exceeded by 25% the average man-hours of buyers' staff time per ten thousand dollars of purchases required by Unit E. On that basis, which one of the following MOST closely approximates the number of buyers' staff man-hours required by Unit E during 2007?
_____ man-hours.

   A. 2,200   B. 2,400   C. 3,000   D. 3,700

50.____

KEY (CORRECT ANSWERS)

1. D	11. C	21. C	31. B	41. C
2. D	12. B	22. A	32. D	42. B
3. C	13. A	23. A	33. B	43. C
4. C	14. B	24. D	34. C	44. A
5. D	15. C	25. C	35. D	45. A
6. A	16. D	26. C	36. B	46. B
7. D	17. A	27. B	37. C	47. C
8. B	18. D	28. A	38. A	48. C
9. C	19. B	29. C	39. B	49. B
10. D	20. A	30. B	40. D	50. B

TEST 2

DIRECTIONS: Each question or incomplete statement is followed by several suggested answers or completions. Select the one that BEST answers the question or completes the statement. *PRINT THE LETTER OF THE CORRECT ANSWER IN THE SPACE AT THE RIGHT.*

1. A certain food is sold in 4 ounce cans at 10 for $3.00 and in 1 pound cans at 3 for $3.00. The SAVINGS in price per ounce by purchasing the food in the larger can is _____ cents/ounce.

    A. 1.59　　　B. 1.05　　　C. 1.25　　　D. 2.04

2. After an article is discounted at 25%, it sells for $375. The ORIGINAL price of the article was

    A. $93.75　　　B. $350　　　C. $375　　　D. $500

3. Assume that you require 1440 pencils, packed 12 to the box, 24 boxes to the carton. Which of the following represents the LOWEST bid for these pencils?

    A. 20¢ per pencil
    B. $65.00 per carton
    C. $2.70 per box less a 4% discount
    D. $400 less a 3% discount

4. If erasers cost 8¢ each for the first 250, 7¢ each for the next 250, and 5¢ for every eraser thereafter, how many erasers may be purchased for $50?

    A. 600　　　B. 750　　　C. 850　　　D. 1000

5. Assume that a buyer saves $14 on the purchase of an item that is discounted at 25%. The amount of money that the buyer must pay for the item is

    A. $42　　　B. $52　　　C. $54　　　D. $56

Questions 6-9.

DIRECTIONS: Questions 6 through 9 are based on the following method of obtaining a reorder point: multiply the monthly rate of consumption by the lead time (in months) and add the minimum balance.

6. If the lead time is one-half month, the minimum balance is 6 units, and the monthly rate of consumption is 4 units, then the reorder point is _____ units.

    A. 4　　　B. 6　　　C. 8　　　D. 12

7. If the reorder point is 25 units, the lead time is 3 months, and the minimum balance is 10 units, then the average monthly rate of consumption is _____ units.

    A. 3　　　B. 5　　　C. 6　　　D. 10

8. If the reorder point is 400 units, the lead time is 2 months, and the monthly rate of consumption is 150 units, then the minimum balance is _____ units.

    A. 50　　　B. 100　　　C. 150　　　D. 200

9. If the reorder point is 75 units, the monthly rate of consumption is 60 units, and the minimum balance is 45 units, then the lead time is _____ month(s).

    A. $\frac{1}{2}$ B. 1   C. 2   D. 4

10. A purchasing office has 4,992 special requisitions to be processed. Working alone, Buyer A could process these in 30 days; working alone, Buyer B could process these in 40 days; working alone, Buyer C could process these in 60 days.
    The LEAST number of days in which Buyers A, B, and C working together can process these 4,992 special requisitions is APPROXIMATELY _____ days.

    A. 14   B. 20   C. 34   D. 45

11. In MOST large manufacturing plants, quality control is a function of the

    A. accounting department
    B. executive staff
    C. personnel department
    D. production department

12. *Net weight* refers to the weight of

    A. an article exclusive of the weights of all packing materials and containers
    B. the shipment at time of packaging including weight of container
    C. the total amount ordered including that which is back-ordered
    D. the total load including all packaging material containers

13. *Invoice* may BEST be defined as

    A. buyer's statement of quantities of merchandise and prices to be furnished by the seller
    B. purchaser's written offer to a supplier formally stating all terms and conditions of a proposed transaction
    C. seller's itemized bill stating prices and quantities of goods delivered and sent to the buyer for payment
    D. sales agreement granting purchaser any discount established by the seller prior to the shipment date

14. Reclaimed property which can be repaired or reused in another manner is MOST likely to be classified as

    A. excess   B. obsolete   C. salvage   D. scrap

15. In preparing specifications for bond and ledger paper, the LEAST important item to be included is

    A. conformity to standards
    B. detailed manufacturing processes
    C. finish and surface
    D. size, weight, and color

16. The standard specifications has LEAST significance for

    A. encouraging substitute bids
    B. enabling the buyer to set quality standards when seeking bids
    C. helping using departments to prepare requisitions
    D. providing the testing laboratory with a basis for comparison of material submitted to it

Questions 17-20.

DIRECTIONS: Questions 17 through 20 refer to types of paper and a description of the quality of each. Match each type of paper in Column I with the appropriate description in Column II.

COLUMN I   COLUMN II

17. Bond   A. Paper used primarily on printing presses   17.____

18. Duplicator   B. Paper with shiny hard surface which does not absorb alcohol well   18.____

19. Mimeograph   C. Somewhat coarse in finish and absorbs ink well   19.____

20. Offset   D. Usually sulphite or rag content and used for correspondence   20.____

21. 1,000 sheets of Sub. 20 paper, size 17" x 22" weighs MOST NEARLY _____ pounds.   21.____

    A. 20   B. 40   C. 60   D. 80

22. In requisitions for lead pencils for general office use, the pencil numbers you should generally expect to appear MOST frequently are the numbers   22.____

    A. 1 and 6   B. 2 and 3   C. 2 and 5   D. 3 and 4

23. Of the following types of lead pencils, the number which represents the HARDEST lead is   23.____

    A. 2B   B. 2H   C. 3B   D. 9H

24. One pound (16 oz.) is equal to _____ grams.   24.____

    A. 100   B. 256   C. 454   D. 1,000

25. How many sheets are there in a ream of paper?   25.____

    A. 200   B. 500   C. 750   D. 1,000

26. The word *prototype* means a(n)   26.____

    A. design of type used in printing
    B. figure or symbol impressed in the manufacture of a product to identify the maker
    C. original or model
    D. method of typewriting

Questions 27-32.

DIRECTIONS: Each of Questions 27 through 32 consists of a statement which contains one word that is incorrectly used because it is not in keeping with the meaning that the quotation is intended to convey. Determine which word is incorrectly used. Then, select from the words lettered A, B, C, or D the word which, when substituted for the incorrectly used word, would BEST help to convey the meaning of the statement.

27. Determining compliance with the required quality is perhaps the most involved and probably one of the most important parts of a good quality-control program.
To function effectively, quality determination should be made immediately on use of the shipment

    A. after
    B. quantity
    C. receipt
    D. system

28. The bidders' list must be sufficient to ensure cooperation. Three is considered the practical minimum number of bidders when the product to be purchased is standardized or the specifications definitely established.
A greater number is desirable, even necessary, when alternates are to be considered, and particularly when specification recommendations are being sought.

    A. competition
    B. lesser
    C. small
    D. unique

29. Purchasing recommends flexibility in specifications to insure wide competition. It discourages the use of commercial standards and tolerances and recommends close adherence to, or allows room for, filling specifications with standard goods. These, of course, are less expensive and are readily available.
In this way, more vendors may be reached.

    A. distribution
    B. encourages
    C. industrial
    D. reliable

30. Purchasing will seek specifications, i.e., accurate descriptions of the material to be purchased, with few tolerances since unnecessary precision is costly.
Further, to permit competition, purchasing will recommend specifications which can be met by many vendors.

    A. absolute
    B. limit
    C. reasonable
    D. prices

31. Inventory turnover rates serve as useful guides in reducing inventories, effecting savings, and influencing procurement schedules.
Careful classification of inventory into perishable and permanent items is necessary after turnover rates are set.

    A. before
    B. helpful
    C. increasing
    D. non-perishable

32. Record keeping of materials in storage is closely associated with the purchasing of the materials. Coordinating stores keeping and purchasing obstructs effective inventory controls and economies.
The storage division can inform purchasing of turnover of items to prevent over- or under-stocking of materials.

    A. authorize
    B. combining
    C. loosely
    D. provides

Questions 33-45.

DIRECTIONS: For Questions 33 through 45, choose from the given classifications the one under which the item is MOST likely to be found in general stock catalogs.

33. *Chisels* may BEST be classified under   33.____

    A. food and condiments
    B. hand tools and accessories
    C. office machines and equipment
    D. stationery supplies

34. *Columnar pads* may BEST be classified under   34.____

    A. drygoods, textiles, and floor covering
    B. hospital and surgical supplies
    C. recreational supplies and equipment
    D. stationery and office supplies

35. *Gingham* may BEST be classified under   35.____

    A. clothing and textiles
    B. hand tools
    C. lighting apparatus
    D. paints and paint ingredients

36. *Trowels* may BEST be classified under   36.____

    A. dry goods and textiles
    B. hand tools and agricultural implements
    C. household supplies
    D. surgical supplies

37. *Collanders* may BEST be classified under   37.____

    A. building materials   B. kitchen utensils
    C. motor vehicle parts   D. plumbing supplies

38. *Litmus paper* may BEST be classified under   38.____

    A. laboratory supplies   B. sewing supplies
    C. stationery and supplies   D. textiles

39. *Pipettes* may BEST be classified under   39.____

    A. hardware
    B. hospital and laboratory supplies
    C. kitchen utensils and tableware
    D. plumbing fixtures and parts

40. *Carbon tetrachloride* may BEST be classified under   40.____

    A. brushes   B. clothing and textiles
    C. drugs and chemicals   D. toilet articles and accessories

41. *Curry powder* may BEST be classified under   41.____

    A. drugs and chemicals
    B. food and condiments
    C. paints and supplies
    D. surgical and dental supplies

42. *Planes* may BEST be classified under   42.____

    A. floor coverings   B. hand tools
    C. household utensils   D. plumbing fixtures

43. *Wing nuts* may BEST be classified under   43.____

    A. food and condiments   B. hardware supplies
    C. household utensils   D. sewing supplies

44. *Chambray* may BEST be classified under   44.____

    A. canned goods, food and misc. groceries
    B. brooms and brushes
    C. drugs and chemicals
    D. dry goods and textiles

45. *Shears* may BEST be classified under   45.____

    A. agricultural implements B. clothing and textiles
    C. electrical parts   D. furniture

46. A BASIC reason for assigning commodity code numbers to purchased and stored items is to   46.____

    A. prevent pilferage
    B. increase the use of mechanized equipment
    C. facilitate ready reference in communications
    D. decrease flexibility of storage areas

47. Which of the following is NOT an important reason for authorizing a purchasing department to control stores?   47.____

    A. Coordination of purchasing and stores may result in economies.
    B. Record keeping of materials in storage is closely associated with the purchase of materials.
    C. The storage division can inform purchasing of turnover of items to prevent overstocking or understocking.
    D. The storerooms will be near the points of use, reducing transportation costs.

48. Any food or drug found by the comptroller to be unwholesome or otherwise unfit for human consumption or use shall NOT be removed by the vendor until it has been examined by the   48.____

    A. department of purchase
    B. environmental protection administration
    C. municipal service administration
    D. department of health

49. Which one of the following is a major function of the board of standardization of the department of purchase?

   A. Determination of locations for major future capital expenditures
   B. Establishment of time limitations for the processing of vouchers for payment
   C. Review and approval of purchasing specifications
   D. Review of maximum floor load limitations in department of purchase storehouses

50. Which one of the following is LEAST likely to be a major commodity grouping utilized by a central purchasing agency?

   A. Automotive equipment and supplies
   B. Condiments and seasonings
   C. Foods, fresh and processed
   D. Fuels, lubricating and plumbing supplies

KEY (CORRECT ANSWERS)

1. C	11. D	21. B	31. A	41. B
2. D	12. A	22. B	32. D	42. B
3. A	13. C	23. D	33. B	43. B
4. B	14. C	24. C	34. D	44. D
5. A	15. B	25. B	35. A	45. A
6. C	16. A	26. C	36. B	46. C
7. B	17. D	27. C	37. B	47. D
8. B	18. B	28. A	38. A	48. D
9. A	19. C	29. B	39. B	49. C
10. A	20. A	30. C	40. C	50. B

EXAMINATION SECTION
TEST 1

DIRECTIONS: Each question or incomplete statement is followed by several suggested answers or completions. Select the one that BEST answers the question or completes the statement. *PRINT THE LETTER OF THE CORRECT ANSWER IN THE SPACE AT THE RIGHT.*

Questions 1-8.

DIRECTIONS: Questions 1 through 8 are to be answered SOLELY on the basis of the following graph.

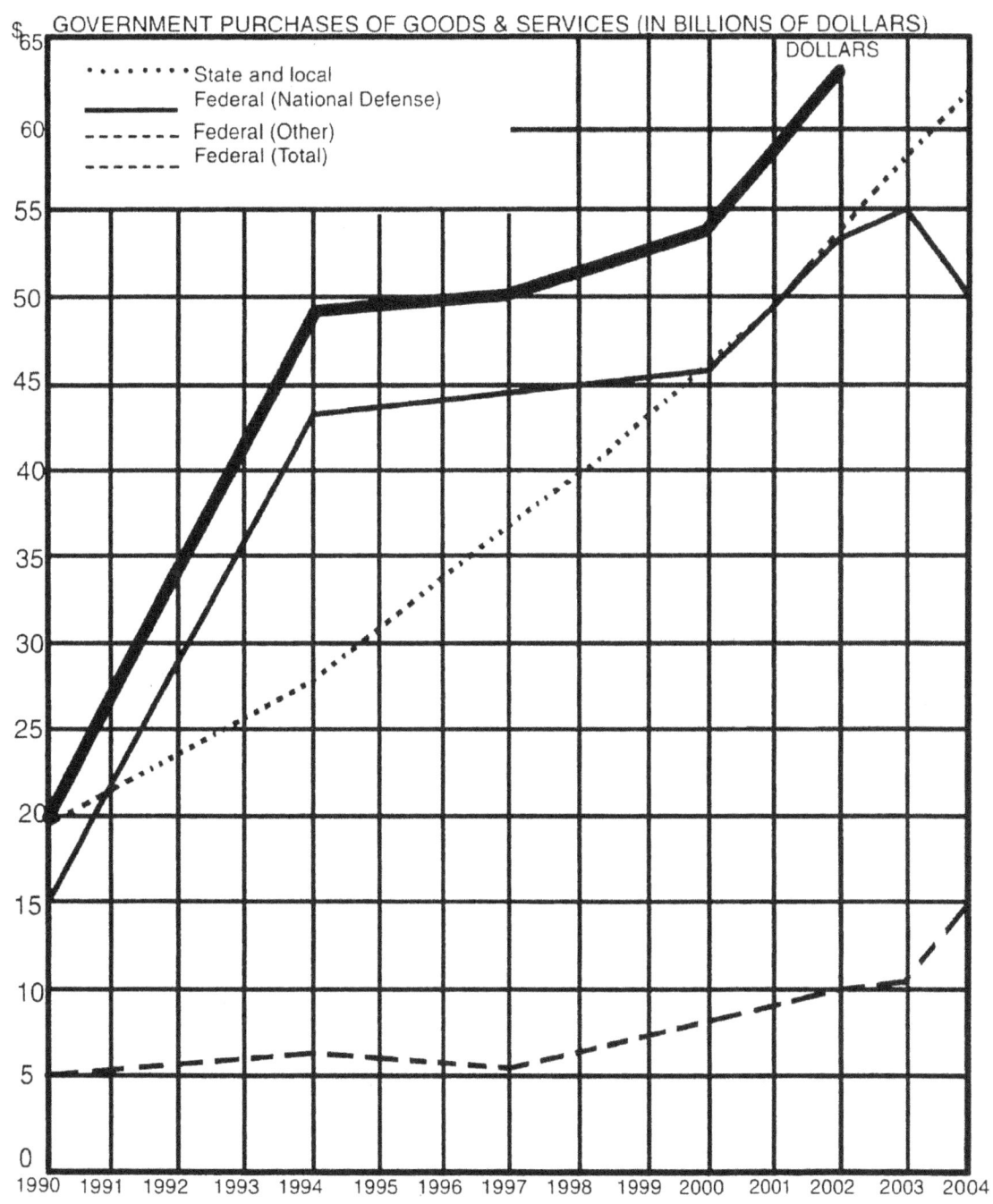

2 (#1)

1. Purchases by the Federal government for non-defense purposes, and purchases by State and local governments comprised the SMALLEST proportion of the total government purchases of goods and services for all purposes in which of the following years?

   A. 1990   B. 1994   C. 1997   D. 2000

2. Which one of the following MOST closely approximates the percentage increase in State and local purchases of goods and services in 2004 as compared with 1990?

   A. 110%   B. 150%   C. 220%   D. 350%

3. Total government purchases of goods and services in 2004 was MOST NEARLY _____ billion dollars.

   A. 80   B. 110   C. 128   D. 144

4. In 2000, purchases made by State and local governments

   A. exceeded Federal government total purchases
   B. exceeded purchases made by them in 1994 by more than 50%
   C. increases less than 10% over 1997
   D. were less than 50% of purchases made by them in 2003

5. Purchases of goods and services for national defense in 1994 by the Federal government was MOST NEARLY

   A. 15% less than the total spent by Federal, State, and local governments for all purposes in 1990
   B. 50% of the total spent by Federal, State, and local governments for all purposes in 1997
   C. four times the amount spent in 1990 for national defense
   D. ten times the amount spent in 1994 by the Federal government for purposes other than national defense

6. In which one of the following years did State and local purchases of goods and services comprise the GREATEST proportion of the total spent by all government jurisdictions?

   A. 1990   B. 1994   C. 1997   D. 2002

7. The dollar increase in purchases of goods and services was LEAST for which one of the following?

   A. State and local governments between 1990 and 1994
   B. State and local governments between 1997 and 2000
   C. Total Federal government between 2000 and 2002
   D. Federal government other than national defense between 2000 and 2003

8. The rate of increase in Federal purchases of goods and services for national defense was GREATEST between which one of the following periods?
   From _____ to _____.

   A. 1994; 1997   B. 1997; 2000
   C. 2000; 2002   D. 2002; 2004

9. A uniform purchasing procedure is desirable in any well managed organization. Of the following, which statement as applied to a uniform purchasing procedure is LEAST valid?
A uniform purchasing procedure

    A. enables suitable documentation of transactions to meet the requirements of any auditing agency
    B. fosters good public relations in the community by giving many vendors an opportunity to bid on items
    C. generally permits low cost paper processing
    D. provides for spot-checking industrial operations so that quality control standards may be changed

9._____

10. A system of progress charting in the procurement of heavy major capital budget equipment would normally be LEAST useful in relation to procuring delivery on target date of which of the following?

    A. Fire Pumpers   B. Garbage Collection Trucks
    C. Mimeograph Machines   D. Police Cars

10._____

11. Standardization has the advantage of lowering the number of purchase orders and the quantity and variety of items to be stored.
The achievement of standardization is MOST generally the objective of

    A. design analysis   B. lead time
    C. perpetual inventory   D. reclamation procedures

11._____

12. Of the following, the LEAST desirable system for identifying standard commodities is the _____ system.

    A. alphabetic   B. alphanumeric
    C. Dewey decimal   D. non-sequential

12._____

13. Which one of the following influences LEAST the price level of commodities?

    A. Current market prices   B. Seasonal trends
    C. Published quotations   D. Storage restrictions

13._____

14. A manufacturer would be BEST advised to bypass the wholesaler or mill supply house when

    A. his product requires specialized selling and service
    B. his product has low value per unit
    C. his product has a demand situation similar to water
    D. he needs widespread distribution to a large number of outlets

14._____

15. The term *cost* usually includes all of the following EXCEPT

    A. any taxes applicable to the job payroll and any payment on bonds specified in the contract
    B. all overhead costs as defined and agreed to
    C. provision to add costs where the final profit margin falls outside limits considered to be reasonable
    D. cost of all material and labor services directly applicable to the job

15._____

16. Convenience goods are generally NOT characterized by which one of the following phrases?

    A. Bought frequently
    B. Minimum effort devoted to purchase
    C. Non-durable
    D. Purchase often postponed until more convenient time

17. Generally, what is the time limit for filing a claim with a carrier for concealed damage?

    A. 15 days   B. 30 days   C. 3 months   D. 1 year

18. Generally, what is the time limit for filing a loss or damage claim with a carrier?

    A. 15 days   B. 3 months   C. 9 months   D. 1 year

19. Of the following, the one which is NOT a reason for NOT making downpayments or progress payments is:

    A. If the item does not perform as required and promised, there may be difficulty in recovering monies paid
    B. Money is tied up before you have use of the item
    C. There is risk of losing the item and part of the payments made if the supplier goes bankrupt
    D. Specially designed machinery and equipment usually cannot be purchased under a contract requiring this method of payment

20. Generally, the impact upon the purchasing function of the use of an automated stock control system is to

    A. eliminate human judgment in determining reorder points
    B. reduce the amount of clerical work required
    C. reduce the need for maintaining safety stock levels
    D. require the drafting of more rigid specifications

21. A buyer who leaves equipment with a skilled worker for repair should be aware that the latter has a right to retain possession of the property until he is paid for the labor or materials he has bestowed on it.
    This right is called a(n)

    A. assignment   B. lien
    C. warrant of attachment   D. bailment

22. Prior to the issuance of orders to new (unlisted) vendors, of the following, it is MOST important to investigate the new vendors'

    A. competence to fulfill their obligations
    B. degree of in-plant mechanization
    C. choice of transportation vehicles
    D. discrimination against potential employees on an age basis

23. Analysis of bids for equipment buying does NOT include analysis of

    A. cost requirements   B. leasing methods
    C. performance efficiency D. specifications

5 (#1)

24. The one of the following which should normally be the MAJOR factor determining the signatory approvals required on a purchase requisition is the   24.____

    A. mode of transportation to be required to deliver the requisitioned items
    B. number of copies of the requisition required
    C. number of different commodity classes included on the requisition
    D. total dollar value of the items on the requisition

25. A statute that requires low dollar limitation on informal bids for open-market purchases is considered by purchasing officials to be generally   25.____

    A. *desirable*; it will increase the efficiency of the purchasing office
    B. *desirable;* it will reduce the incurrence of additional costs
    C. *undesirable*; it will cause unnecessary delays
    D. *undesirable;* it will result in a tendency to bypass local sources of supply

26. In preparing an annual requirement contract, the estimated quantity to be purchased should GENERALLY be   26.____

    A. inflated, in order to receive the lowest price possible
    B. comparable to the quantity purchased the previous year, unless it is expected that a greater quantity will be required for the ensuing year
    C. reduced, in order to allow for additional small orders in case of a drop in prices
    D. related to the quality specifications of the item

27. The MAJOR purpose of a price escalator clause in a contract is to   27.____

    A. define the rights of the seller and buyer if the seller cannot deliver merchandise of the quality, quantity, and at the price specified
    B. enable the buyer and seller to allocate elements of cost risk equitably between them
    C. enable the buyer to cancel the contract if costs of production exceed prices agreed upon
    D. ward off changes in price anticipated as a result of pending legislation or governmental regulation

28. Sales terms to Gideonburg, Ohio plant state that price is F.O.B. Dayton, Ohio, freight equalized with Akron, Ohio. At the buyer's request, freight is prepaid to New York City. In absence of any other provision in the agreement, titles will pass to the buyer at   28.____

    A. Akron   B. Dayton
    C. Gideonburg   D. New York City

29. A seller makes a false statement to a buyer of a material fact regarding certain merchandise which he is offering for sale. The statement is made with intent to deceive the buyer and induces him to enter into a contract which, had he not been misled, he would not have entered into. According to the above statement, which of the following statements is MOST valid?
    The   29.____

    A. seller is guilty of misrepresentation which justifies rescission of the contract
    B. buyer may not have the contract rescinded, though
    C. he is entitled to receive compensation for any losses he has sustained

D. seller may enforce the contract if he can prove that his merchandise is as good as or better than the merchandise contracted for
E. buyer is guilty of misplaced confidence; he takes the risk of quality unless he protects himself by a warranty beforehand

30. Assume that you require 4 tons of fertilizer. The fertilizer is packed in 100 pound bags. Which of the following represents the LOWEST bid for the fertilizer?

   A. 6¢ per pound
   B. $5.50 per bag
   C. $7.00 for each of the first 30 bags; $5.00 for each bag thereafter
   D. $500.00 less discount

31. Assume pencils are packed 5 gross to the case. A buyer requires 3800 pencils each for three departments and 2700 pencils for another department. Assume that the vendor will ship unbroken cases only directly to each department.
   How many cases should he buy?

   A. 21   B. 22   C. 48   D. 49

32. Printing from raised surface is done by which printing process?

   A. Debossing   B. Letterpress
   C. Offset lithography D. Rotogravure

33. Of the following, the topic which is LEAST appropriate in a governmental purchasing manual is

   A. Buying for Employees   B. Ethics
   C. Training   D. Vendor Contacts

34. Which one of the following is LEAST appropriate as a program objective for a central purchasing agency?

   A. Decreasing the degree of mechanization of storehouse operations
   B. Developing a more meaningful training program for the buying staff
   C. Updating and delineating purchasing procedure for use by the agency's own staff and by using agency personnel concerned with procurement
   D. Relieving buyers of clerical duties so that they may concentrate more on the elevation of the quality and scope of purchasing activities

35. The use of an automated inventory control system GENERALLY results in

   A. an increase in the number of items kept in inventory
   B. greater utilization of available warehouse storage space
   C. the availability of more accurate perpetual inventory data
   D. the elimination of the need for physical inventories

36. For a buyer in charge of a section to ask occasionally the opinion of a subordinate concerning a buying problem is

   A. *desirable;* but it would be even better if the subordinate were consulted routinely on every buying problem
   B. *desirable;* subordinates may make good suggestions and will be pleased by being consulted

C. *undesirable;* subordinates may be resentful if their advice is not followed
D. *undesirable;* the buyer should not attempt to shift his responsibilities to subordinates

37. Generally, it is considered desirable practice to maintain stock at a three months level of supply.
Under what circumstances would it be MOST desirable to reduce stock levels to a one month period?

    A. Discounts when buying larger quantities
    B. Few obsolete items
    C. Rapid deterioration of items
    D. Rising prices

37._____

38. You find that delivery of a certain item cannot possibly be made to a using agency by the date the using agency requested.
Of the following, the MOST advisable course of action for you to take FIRST is to

    A. cancel the order and inform the using agency
    B. discuss the problem with the using agency
    C. notify the using agency to obtain the item through direct purchase
    D. schedule the delivery for the earliest possible date

38._____

39. Of the following classes of supplies, the one which you would expect to have the HIGHEST safety stock level is

    A. foods
    B. office machines
    C. pharmaceuticals and drugs
    D. spare parts

39._____

40. When a buyer delegates some of his work to a subordinate, the

    A. buyer retains final responsibility for the work
    B. buyer should not check on the work until it has been completed
    C. subordinate assumes full responsibility for the successful completion of the work
    D. subordinate is likely to lose interest and get less satisfaction from the work

40._____

KEY (CORRECT ANSWERS)

1.	B	11.	A	21.	B	31.	B
2.	C	12.	D	22.	A	32.	B
3.	C	13.	D	23.	B	33.	A
4.	B	14.	A	24.	D	34.	A
5.	B	15.	C	25.	C	35.	C
6.	A	16.	D	26.	B	36.	B
7.	D	17.	A	27.	B	37.	C
8.	C	18.	C	28.	B	38.	B
9.	D	19.	D	29.	A	39.	D
10.	C	20.	B	30.	B	40.	A

EXAMINATION SECTION
TEST 1

DIRECTIONS: Each question or incomplete statement is followed by several suggested answers or completions. Select the one that BEST answers the question or completes the statement. *PRINT THE LETTER OF THE CORRECT ANSWER IN THE SPACE AT THE RIGHT.*

1. Of the following, the one MOST important quality required of a good supervisor is
    A. ambition   B. leadership   C. friendliness   D. popularity

    1.____

2. It is often said that a supervisor can delegate authority but never responsibility. This means MOST NEARLY that
    A. a supervisor must do his own work if he expects it to be done properly
    B. a supervisor can assign someone else to do his work, but in the last analysis, the supervisor himself must take the blame for any actions followed
    C. authority and responsibility are two separate things that cannot be borne by the same person
    D. it is better for a supervisor never to delegate his authority

    2.____

3. One of your men who is a habitual complainer asks you to grant him a minor privilege.
   Before granting or denying such a request, you should consider
    A. the merits of the case
    B. that it is good for group morale to grant a request of this nature
    C. the man's seniority
    D. that to deny such a request will lower your standing with the men

    3.____

4. A supervisory practice on the part of a foreman which is MOST likely to lead to confusion and inefficiency is for him to
    A. give orders verbally directly to the man assigned to the job
    B. issue orders only in writing
    C. follow up his orders after issuing them
    D. relay his orders to the men through co-workers

    4.____

5. It would be POOR supervision on a foreman's part if he
    A. asked an experienced maintainer for his opinion on the method of doing a special job
    B. make it a policy to avoid criticizing a man in front of his co-workers
    C. consulted his assistant supervisor on unusual problems
    D. allowed a cooling-off period of several days before giving one of his men a deserved reprimand

    5.____

6. Of the following behavior characteristics of a supervisor, the one that is MOST likely to lower the morale of the men he supervises is
   A. diligence
   B. favoritism
   C. punctuality
   D. thoroughness

7. Of the following, the BEST method of getting an employee who is not working up to his capacity to produce more work is to
   A. have another employee criticize his production
   B. privately criticize his production but encourage him to produce more
   C. criticize his production before his associates
   D. criticize his production and threaten to fire him

8. Of the following, the BEST thing for a supervisor to do when a subordinate has done a very good job is to
   A. tell him to take it easy
   B. praise his work
   C. reduce his workload
   D. say nothing because he may become conceited

9. Your orders to your crew are MOST likely to be followed if you
   A. explain the reasons for these orders
   B. warn that all violators will be punished
   C. promise easy assignments to those who follow these orders best
   D. say that they are for the good of the department

10. In order to be a good supervisor, you should
    A. impress upon your men that you demand perfection in their work at all times
    B. avoid being blamed for your crew's mistakes
    C. impress your superior with your ability
    D. see to it that your men get what they are entitled to

11. In giving instructions to a crew, you should
    A. speak in as loud a tone as possible
    B. speak in a coaxing, persuasive manner
    C. speak quietly, clearly, and courteously
    D. always use the word *please* when giving instructions

12. Of the following factors, the one which is LEAST important in evaluating an employee and his work is his
    A. dependability
    B. quantity of work done
    C. quality of work done
    D. education and training

13. When a District Superintendent first assumes his command, it is LEAST important for him at the beginning to observe
    A. how his equipment is designed and its adaptability
    B. how to reorganize the district for greater efficiency
    C. the capabilities of the men in the district
    D. the methods of operation being employed

14. When making an inspection of one of the buildings under your supervision, the BEST procedure to follow in making a record of the inspection is to
    A. return immediately to the office and write a report from memory
    B. write down all the important facts during or as soon as you complete the inspection
    C. fix in your mind all important facts so that you can repeat them from memory if necessary
    D. fix in your mind all important facts so that you can make out your report at the end of the day

15. Assume that your superior has directed you to make certain changes in your established procedure. After using this modified procedure on several occasions, you find that the original procedure was distinctly superior and you wish to return to it.
    You should
    A. let your superior find this out for himself
    B. simply change back to the original procedure
    C. compile definite data and information to prove your case to your superior
    D. persuade one of the more experienced workers to take this matter up with your superior

16. An inspector visited a large building under construction. He inspected the soil lines at 9 A.M., water lines at 10 A.M., fixtures at 11 A.M., and did his office work in the afternoon. He followed the same pattern daily for weeks.
    This procedure was
    A. *good*, because it was methodical and he did not miss anything
    B. *good*, because it gave equal time to all phases of the plumbing
    C. *bad*, because not enough time was devoted to fixtures
    D. *bad*, because the tradesmen knew when the inspection would occur

17. Assume that one of the foremen in a training course, which you are conducting, proposes a poor solution for a maintenance problem.
    Of the following, the BEST course of action for you to take is to
    A. accept the solution tentatively and correct it during the next class meeting
    B. point out all the defects of this proposed solution and wait until somebody thinks of a better solution
    C. try to get the class to reject this proposed solution and develop a better solution
    D. let the matter pass since somebody will present a better solution as the class work proceeds

18. As a supervisor, you should be seeking ways to improve the efficiency of shop operations by means such as changing established work procedures.
    The following are offered as possible actions that you should consider in changing established work procedures:
    I. Make changes only when your foremen agree to them
    II. Discuss changes with your supervisor before putting them into practice

III. Standardize any operation which is performed on a continuing basis
IV. Make changes quickly and quietly in order to avoid dissent
V. Secure expert guidance before instituting unfamiliar procedures

Of the following suggested answers, the one that describes the actions to be taken to change established work procedures is

A. I, IV, V   B. II, III, V   C. III, IV, V   D. All of the above

19. A supervisor determined that a foreman, without informing his superior, delegated responsibility for checking time cards to a member of his gang. The supervisor then called the foreman into his office where he reprimanded the foreman.
This action of the supervisor in reprimanding the foreman was
    A. *proper*, because the checking of time cards is the foreman's responsibility and should not be delegated
    B. *proper*, because the foreman did not ask the supervisor for permission to delegate responsibility
    C. *improper*, because the foreman may no longer take the initiative in solving future problems
    D. *improper*, because the supervisor is interfering in a function which is not his responsibility

20. A capable supervisor should check all operations under his control.
Of the following, the LEAST important reason for doing this is to make sure that
    A. operations are being performed as scheduled
    B. he personally observes all operations at all times
    C. all the operations are still needed
    D. his manpower is being utilized efficiently

21. A supervisor makes it a practice to apply fair and firm discipline in all cases of rule infractions, including those of a minor nature.
This practice should PRIMARILY be considered
    A. *bad*, since applying discipline for minor violations is a waste of time
    B. *good*, because not applying discipline for minor infractions can lead to a more serious erosion of discipline
    C. *bad*, because employees do not like to be disciplined for minor violations of the rules
    D. *good*, because violating any rule can cause a dangerous situation to occur

22. A maintainer would PROPERLY consider it poor supervisory practice for a foreman to consult with him on
    A. which of several repair jobs should be scheduled first
    B. how to cope with personal problems at home
    C. whether the neatness of his headquarters can be improved
    D. how to express a suggestion which the maintainer plans to submit formally

23. Assume that you have determined that the work of one of your foremen and the men he supervises is consistently behind schedule. When you discuss this situation with the foreman, he tells you that his men are poor workers and then complains that he must spend all of his time checking on their work.
The following actions are offered for your consideration as possible ways of solving the problem of poor performance of the foreman and his men:
   I. Review the work standards with the foreman and determine whether they are realistic.
   II. Tell the foreman that you will recommend him for the foreman's training course for retraining.
   III. Ask the foreman for the names of the maintainers and then replace them as soon as possible.
   IV. Tell the foreman that you expect him to meet a satisfactory level of performance.
   V. Tell the foreman to insist that his men work overtime to catch up to the schedule.
   VI. Tell the foreman to review the type and amount of training he has given the maintainers.
   VII. Tell the foreman that he will be out of a job if he does not produce on schedule.
   VIII. Avoid all criticism of the foreman and his methods.
   Which of the following suggested answers CORRECTLY lists the proper actions to be taken to solve the problem of poor performance of the foreman and his men?
   A. I, II, IV, VI   B. I, III, V, VII   C. II, III, VI, VIII   D. IV, V, VI, VIII

24. When a conference or a group discussion is tending to turn into a *bull session* without constructive purpose, the BEST action to take is to
   A. reprimand the leader of the bull session
   B. redirect the discussion to the business at hand
   C. dismiss the meeting and reschedule it for another day
   D. allow the bull session to continue

25. Assume that you have been assigned responsibility for a program in which a high production rate is mandatory. From past experience, you know that your foremen do not perform equally well in the various types of jobs given to them. Which of the following methods should you use in selecting foremen for the specific types of work involved in the program?
   A. Leave the method of selecting foremen to your supervisor
   B. Assign each foreman to the work he does best
   C. Allow each foreman to choose his own job
   D. Assign each foreman to a job which will permit him to improve his own abilities

KEY (CORRECT ANSWERS)

1.	B	11.	C
2.	B	12.	D
3.	A	13.	B
4.	D	14.	B
5.	D	15.	C
6.	B	16.	D
7.	B	17.	C
8.	B	18.	B
9.	A	19.	A
10.	D	20.	B

21.	B
22.	A
23.	A
24.	B
25.	B

TEST 2

DIRECTIONS: Each question or incomplete statement is followed by several suggested answers or completions. Select the one that BEST answers the question or completes the statement. *PRINT THE LETTER OF THE CORRECT ANSWER IN THE SPACE AT THE RIGHT.*

1. A foreman who is familiar with modern management principles should know that the one of the following requirements of an administrator which is LEAST important is his ability to
   A. coordinate work
   B. plan, organize, and direct the work under his control
   C. cooperate with others
   D. perform the duties of the employees under his jurisdiction

   1._____

2. When subordinates request his advice in solving problems encountered in their work, a certain chief occasionally answers the request by first asking the subordinate what he thinks should be done.
   This action by the chief is, on the whole,
   A. *desirable*, because it stimulates subordinates to give more thought to the solution of problems encountered
   B. *undesirable*, because it discourages subordinates from asking questions
   C. *desirable*, because it discourages subordinates from asking questions
   D. *undesirable*, because it undermines the confidence of subordinates in the ability of their supervisor

   2._____

3. Of the following factors that may be considered by a unit head in dealing with the tardy subordinate, the one which should be given LEAST consideration is the
   A. frequency with which the employee is tardy
   B. effect of the employee's tardiness upon the work of other employees
   C. willingness of the employee to work overtime when necessary
   D. cause of the employee's tardiness

   3._____

4. The MOST important requirement of a good inspectional report is that it should be
   A. properly addressed   B. lengthy
   C. clear and brief   D. spelled correctly

   4._____

5. Building superintendents frequently inquire about departmental inspectional procedures.
   Of the following, it is BEST to
   A. advise them to write to the department for an official reply
   B. refuse as the inspectional procedure is a restricted matter
   C. briefly explain the procedure to them
   D. avoid the inquiry by changing the subject

   5._____

6. Reprimanding a crew member before other workers is a
   A. *good* practice; the reprimand serves as a warning to the other workers
   B. *bad* practice; people usually resent criticism made in public
   C. *good* practice; the other workers will realize that the supervisor is fair
   D. *bad* practice; the other workers will take sides in the dispute

7. Of the following actions, the one which is LEAST likely to promote good work is for the group leader to
   A. praise workers for doing a good job
   B. call attention to the opportunities for promotion for better workers
   C. threaten to recommend discharge of workers who are below standard
   D. put into practice any good suggestion made by crew members

8. A supervisor notices that a member of his crew has skipped a routine step in his job.
   Of the following, the BEST action for the supervisor to take is to
   A. promptly question the worker about the incident
   B. immediately assign another man to complete the job
   C. bring up the incident the next time the worker asks for a favor
   D. say nothing about the incident but watch the worker carefully in the future

9. Assume you have been told to show a new worker how to operate a piece of equipment.
   Your FIRST step should be to
   A. ask the worker if he has any questions about the equipment
   B. permit the worker to operate the equipment himself while you carefully watch to prevent damage
   C. demonstrate the operation of the equipment for the worker
   D. have the worker read an instruction booklet on the maintenance of the equipment

10. Whenever a new man was assigned to his crew, the supervisor would introduce him to all other crew members, take him on a tour of the plant, tell him about bus schedules and places to eat.
    This practice is
    A. *good*; the new man is made to feel welcome
    B. *bad*; supervisors should not interfere in personal matters
    C. *good*; the new man knows that he can bring his personal problems to the supervisor
    D. *bad*; work time should not be spent on personal matters

11. The MOST important factor in successful leadership is the ability to
    A. obtain instant obedience to all orders
    B. establish friendly personal relations with crew members
    C. avoid disciplining crew members
    D. make crew members want to do what should be done

12. Explaining the reasons for departmental procedure to workers tends to
    A. waste time which should be used for productive purposes
    B. increase their interest in their work
    C. make them more critical of departmental procedures
    D. confuse them

13. If you want a job done well do it yourself.
    For a supervisor to follow this advice would be
    A. *good*; a supervisor is responsible for the work of his crew
    B. *bad*; a supervisor should train his men, not do their work
    C. *good*; a supervisor should be skilled in all jobs assigned to his crew
    D. *bad*; a supervisor loses respect when he works with his hands

14. When a supervisor discovers a mistake in one of the jobs for which his crew is responsible, it is MOST important for him to find out
    A. whether anybody else knows about the mistake
    B. who was to blame for the mistake
    C. how to prevent similar mistakes in the future
    D. whether similar mistakes occurred in the past

15. A supervisor who has to explain a new procedure to his crew should realize that questions from the crew USUALLY show that they
    A. are opposed to the new practice
    B. are completely confused by the explanation
    C. need more training in the new procedure
    D. are interested in the explanation

16. A good way for a supervisor to retain the confidence of his or her employees is to
    A. say as little as possible
    B. check work frequently
    C. make no promises unless they will be fulfilled
    D. never hesitate in giving an answer to any question

17. Good supervision is ESSENTIALLY a matter of
    A. patience in supervising workers   B. care in selecting workers
    C. skill in human relations   D. fairness in disciplining workers

18. It is MOST important for an employee who has been assigned a monotonous task to
    A. perform this task before doing other work
    B. ask another employee to help
    C. perform this task only after all other work has been completed
    D. take measures to prevent mistakes in performing the task

19. One of your employees has violated a minor agency regulation.
    The FIRST thing you should do is
    A. warn the employee that you will have to take disciplinary action if it should happen again
    B. ask the employee to explain his or her actions
    C. inform your supervisor and wait for advice
    D. write a memo describing the incident and place it in the employee's personnel file

20. One of your employees tells you that he feels you give him much more work than the other employees, and he is having trouble meeting your deadlines.
    You should
    A. ask if he has been under a lot of non-work related stress lately
    B. review his recent assignments to determine if he is correct
    C. explain that this is a busy time, but you are dividing the work equally
    D. tell him that he is the most competent employee and that is why he receives more work

21. A supervisor assigns one of his crew to complete a portion of a job. A short time later, the supervisor notices that the portion has not been completed.
    Of the following, the BEST way for the supervisor to handle this is to
    A. ask the crew member why he has not completed the assignment
    B. reprimand the crew member for not obeying orders
    C. assign another crew member to complete the assignment
    D. complete the assignment himself

22. Supposes that a member of your crew complains that you are *playing favorites* in assigning work.
    Of the following, the BEST method of handling the complaint is to
    A. deny it and refuse to discuss the matter with the worker
    B. take the opportunity to tell the worker what is wrong with his work
    C. ask the worker for examples to prove his point and try to clear up any misunderstanding
    D. promise to be more careful in making assignments in the future

23. A member of your crew comes to you with a complaint. After discussing the matter with him, it is clear that you have convinced him that his complaint was not justified.
    At this point, you should
    A. permit him to drop the matter
    B. make him admit his error
    C. pretend to see some justification in his complaint
    D. warn him against making unjustified complaints

24. Suppose that a supervisor has in his crew an older man who works rather slowly. In other respects, this man is a good worker; he is seldom absent, works carefully, never loafs, and is cooperative.

The BEST way for the supervisor to handle this worker is to
   A. try to get him to work faster and less carefully
   B. give him the most disagreeable job
   C. request that he be given special training
   D. permit him to work at his own speed

25. Suppose that a member of your crew comes to you with a suggestion he thinks will save time in doing a job. You realize immediately that it won't work.
    Under these circumstances, your BEST action would be to
    A. thank the worker for the suggestion and forget about it
    B. explain to the worker why you think it won't work
    C. tell the worker to put the suggestion in writing
    D. ask the other members of your crew to criticize the suggestion

25.____

KEY (CORRECT ANSWERS)

1.	D	11.	D
2.	A	12.	B
3.	C	13.	B
4.	C	14.	C
5.	C	15.	D
6.	B	16.	C
7.	C	17.	C
8.	A	18.	D
9.	C	19.	B
10.	A	20.	B

21.	A
22.	C
23.	A
24.	D
25.	B

READING COMPREHENSION
UNDERSTANDING AND INTERPRETING WRITTEN MATERIAL
EXAMINATION SECTION
TEST 1

DIRECTIONS: Each question or incomplete statement is followed by several suggested answers or completions. Select the one that BEST answers the question or completes the statement. *PRINT THE LETTER OF THE CORRECT ANSWER IN THE SPACE AT THE RIGHT.*

Questions 1-3.

DIRECTIONS: Questions 1 through 3 are to be answered SOLELY on the basis of the following statement.

The equipment in a mailroom may include a mail metering machine. This machine simultaneously stamps, postmarks, seals, and counts letters as fast as the operator can feed them. It can also print the proper postage directly on a gummed strip to be affixed to bulky items. It is equipped with a meter which is removed from the machine and sent to the postmaster to be set for a given number of stampings of any denomination. The setting of the meter must be paid for in advance. One of the advantages of metered mail is that it bypasses the cancellation operation and thereby facilitates handling by the post office. Mail metering also makes the pilfering of stamps impossible, but does not prevent the passage of personal mail in company envelopes through the meters unless there is established a rigid control or censorship over outgoing mail.

1. According to this statement, the postmaster

   A. is responsible for training new clerks in the use of mail metering machines
   B. usually recommends that both large and small firms adopt the use of mail metering machines
   C. is responsible for setting the meter to print a fixed number of stampings
   D. examines the mail metering machine to see that they are properly installed in the mailroom

2. According to this statement, the use of mail metering machines

   A. requires the employment of more clerks in a mailroom than does the use of postage stamps
   B. interferes with the handling of large quantities of outgoing mail
   C. does not prevent employees from sending their personal letters at company expense
   D. usually involves smaller expenditures for mailroom equipment than does the use of postage stamps

3. On the basis of this statement, it is MOST accurate to state that

   A. mail metering machines are often used for opening envelopes
   B. postage stamps are generally used when bulky packages are to be mailed
   C. the use of metered mail tends to interfere with rapid mail handling by the post office
   D. mail metering machines can seal and count letters at the same time

1.____

2.____

3.____

Questions 4-5.

DIRECTIONS: Questions 4 and 5 are to be answered SOLELY on the basis of the following statement.

Forms are printed sheets of paper on which information is to be entered. While what is printed on the form is most important, the kind of paper used in making the form is also important. The kind of paper should be selected with regard to the use to which the form will be subjected. Printing a form on an unnecessarily expensive grade of papers is wasteful. On the other hand, using too cheap or flimsy a form can materially interfere with satisfactory performance of the work the form is being planned to do. Thus, a form printed on both sides normally requires a heavier paper than a form printed only on one side. Forms to be used as permanent records, or which are expected to have a very long life in files, requires a quality of paper which will not disintegrate or discolor with age. A form which will go through a great deal of handling requires a strong, tough paper, while thinness is a necessary qualification where the making of several copies of a form will be required.

4. According to this statement, the type of paper used for making forms 4.___

    A. should be chosen in accordance with the use to which the form will be put
    B. should be chosen before the type of printing to be used has been decided upon
    C. is as important as the information which is printed on it
    D. should be strong enough to be used for any purpose

5. According to this statement, forms that are 5.___

    A. printed on both sides are usually economical and desirable
    B. to be filed permanently should not deteriorate as time goes on
    C. expected to last for a long time should be handled carefully
    D. to be filed should not be printed on inexpensive paper

Questions 6-8.

DIRECTIONS: Questions 6 through 8 are to be answered SOLELY on the basis of the following paragraph.

The increase in the number of public documents in the last two centuries closely matches the increase in population in the United States. The great number of public documents has become a serious threat to their usefulness. It is necessary to have programs which will reduce the number of public documents that are kept and which will, at the same time, assure keeping those that have value. Such programs need a great deal of thought to have any success.

6. According to the above paragraph, public documents may be LESS useful if 6.___

    A. the files are open to the public
    B. the record room is too small
    C. the copying machine is operated only during normal working hours
    D. too many records are being kept

7. According to the above paragraph, the growth of the population in the United States has matched the growth in the quantity of public documents for a period of MOST NEARLY _____ years.   7.____

   A. 50   B. 100   C. 200   D. 300

8. According to the above paragraph, the increased number of public documents has made it necessary to   8.____

   A. find out which public documents are worth keeping
   B. reduce the great number of public documents by decreasing government services
   C. eliminate the copying of all original public documents
   D. avoid all new copying devices

Questions 9-10.

DIRECTIONS: Questions 9 and 10 are to be answered SOLELY on the basis of the following paragraph.

The work goals of an agency can best be reached if the employees understand and agree with these goals. One way to gain such understanding and agreement is for management to encourage and seriously consider suggestions from employees in the setting of agency goals.

9. On the basis of the above paragraph, the BEST way to achieve the work goals of an agency is to   9.____

   A. make certain that employees work as hard as possible
   B. study the organizational structure of the agency
   C. encourage employees to think seriously about the agency's problems
   D. stimulate employee understanding of the work goals

10. On the basis of the above paragraph, understanding and agreement with agency goals can be gained by   10.____

    A. allowing the employees to set agency goals
    B. reaching agency goals quickly
    C. legislative review of agency operations
    D. employee participation in setting agency goals

Questions 11-13.

DIRECTIONS: Questions 11 through 13 are to be answered SOLELY on the basis of the following paragraph.

In order to organize records properly, it is necessary to start from their very beginning and trace each copy of the record to find out how it is used, how long it is used, and what may finally be done with it. Although several copies of the record are made, one copy should be marked as the copy of record. This is the formal legal copy, held to meet the requirements of the law. The other copies may be retained for brief periods for reference purposes, but these copies should not be kept after their usefulness as reference ends. There is another reason for tracing records through the office and that is to determine how long it takes the copy of record to reach the central file. The copy of record must not be kept longer than necessary by the section of the office which has prepared it, but should be sent to the central file as soon as possible so that it can be available to the various sections of the office. The central file can make the copy of record available to the various sections of the office at an early date only if it arrives at the central file as quickly as possible. Just as soon as its immediate or active service period is ended, the copy of record should be removed from the central file and put into the inactive file in the office to be stored for whatever length of time may be necessary to meet legal requirements, and then destroyed.

11. According to the above paragraph, a reason for tracing records through an office is to   11._____

    A. determine how long the central file must keep the records
    B. organize records properly
    C. find out how many copies of each record are required
    D. identify the copy of record

12. According to the above paragraph, in order for the central file to have the copy of record available as soon as possible for the various sections of the office, it is MOST important that the   12._____

    A. copy of record to be sent to the central file meets the requirements of the law
    B. copy of record is not kept in the inactive file too long
    C. section preparing the copy of record does not unduly delay in sending it to the central file
    D. central file does not keep the copy of record beyond its active service period

13. According to the above paragraph, the length of time a copy of a record is kept in the inactive file of an office depends CHIEFLY on the   13._____

    A. requirements of the law
    B. length of time that is required to trace the copy of record through the office
    C. use that is made of the copy of record
    D. length of the period that the copy of record is used for reference purposes

Questions 14-16.

DIRECTIONS: Questions 14 through 16 are to be answered SOLELY on the basis of the following paragraph.

The office was once considered as nothing more than a focal point of internal and external correspondence. It was capable only of dispatching a few letters upon occasion and of preparing records of little practical value. Under such a concept, the vitality of the office force was impaired. Initiative became stagnant, and the lot of the office worker was not likely to be a happy one. However, under the new concept of office management, the possibilities of waste and mismanagement in office operation are now fully recognized, as are the possibilities for the modern office to assist in the direction and control of business operations. Fortunately, the modern concept of the office as a centralized service-rendering unit is gaining ever greater acceptance in today's complex business world, for without the modern office, the production wheels do not turn and the distribution of goods and services is not possible.

14. According to the above paragraph, the fundamental difference between the old and the new concept of the office is the change in the

   A. accepted functions of the office
   B. content and the value of the records kept
   C. office methods and systems
   D. vitality and morale of the office force

14._____

15. According to the above paragraph, an office operated today under the old concept of the office MOST likely would

   A. make older workers happy in their jobs
   B. be part of an old thriving business concern
   C. have a passive role in the conduct of a business enterprise
   D. attract workers who do not believe in modern methods

15._____

16. Of the following, the MOST important implication of the above paragraph is that a present-day business organization cannot function effectively without the

   A. use of modern office equipment
   B. participation and cooperation of the office
   C. continued modernization of office procedures
   D. employment of office workers with skill and initiative

16._____

Questions 17-20.

DIRECTIONS: Questions 17 through 20 are to be answered SOLELY on the basis of the following paragraph.

A report is frequently ineffective because the person writing it is not fully acquainted with all the necessary details before he actually starts to construct the report. All details pertaining to the subject should be known before the report is started. If the essential facts are not known, they should be investigated. It is wise to have essential facts written down rather than to depend too much on memory, especially if the facts pertain to such matters as amounts, dates, names of persons, or other specific data. When the necessary information has been gathered, the general plan and content of the report should be thought out before the writing is actually begun. A person with little or no experience in writing reports may find that it is wise to make a brief outline. Persons with more experience should not need a written outline, but they should make mental notes of the steps they are to follow. If writing reports without dictation is a regular part of an office worker's duties, he should set aside a certain time during the day when he is least likely to be interrupted. That may be difficult, but in most offices there are certain times in the day when the callers, telephone calls, and other interruptions are not numerous. During those times, it is best to write reports that need undivided concentration. Reports that are written amid a series of interruptions may be poorly done.

17. Before starting to write an effective report, it is necessary to

   A. memorize all specific information
   B. disregard ambiguous data
   C. know all pertinent information
   D. develop a general plan

17._____

18. Reports dealing with complex and difficult material should be

    A. prepared and written by the supervisor of the unit
    B. written when there is the least chance of interruption
    C. prepared and written as part of regular office routine
    D. outlined and then dictated

19. According to the paragraph, employees with no prior familiarity in writing reports may find it helpful to

    A. prepare a brief outline
    B. mentally prepare a synopsis of the report's content
    C. have a fellow employee help in writing the report
    D. consult previous reports

20. In writing a report, needed information which is unclear should be

    A. disregarded   B. memorized
    C. investigated   D. gathered

Questions 21-25.

DIRECTIONS: Questions 21 through 25 are to be answered SOLELY on the basis of the following passage.

Positive discipline minimizes the amount of personal supervision required and aids in the maintenance of standards. When a new employee has been properly introduced and carefully instructed, when he has come to know the supervisor and has confidence in the supervisor's ability to take care of him, when he willingly cooperates with the supervisor, that employee has been under positive discipline and can be put on his own to produce the quantity and quality of work desired. Negative discipline, the fear of transfer to a less desirable location, for example, to a limited extent may restrain certain individuals from overt violation of rules and regulations governing attendance and conduct which in governmental agencies are usually on at least an agency-wide basis. Negative discipline may prompt employees to perform according to certain rules to avoid a penalty such as, for example, docking for tardiness.

21. According to the above passage, it is reasonable to assume that in the area of discipline, the first-line supervisor in a governmental agency has GREATER scope for action in

    A. *positive* discipline, because negative discipline is largely taken care of by agency rules and regulations
    B. *negative* discipline, because rules and procedures are already fixed and the supervisor can rely on them
    C. *positive* discipline, because the supervisor is in a position to recommend transfers
    D. *negative* discipline, because positive discipline is reserved for people on a higher supervisory level

22. In order to maintain positive discipline of employees under his supervision, it is MOST important for a supervisor to

    A. assure each employee that he has nothing to worry about
    B. insist at the outset on complete cooperation from employees

C. be sure that each employee is well trained in his job
D. inform new employees of the penalties for not meeting standards

23. According to the above passage, a feature of negative discipline is that it   23._____

    A. may lower employee morale
    B. may restrain employees from disobeying the rules
    C. censures equal treatment of employees
    D. tends to create standards for quality of work

24. A REASONABLE conclusion based on the above passage is that positive discipline benefits a supervisor because   24._____

    A. he can turn over orientation and supervision of a new employee to one of his subordinates
    B. subordinates learn to cooperate with one another when working on an assignment
    C. it is easier to administer
    D. it cuts down, in the long run, on the amount of time the supervisor needs to spend on direct supervision

25. Based on the above passage, it is REASONABLE to assume, that an important difference between positive discipline and negative discipline is that positive discipline   25._____

    A. is concerned with the quality of work and negative discipline with the quantity of work
    B. leads to a more desirable basis for motivation of the employee
    C. is more likely to be concerned with agency rules and regulations
    D. uses fear while negative discipline uses penalties to prod employees to adequate performance

KEY (CORRECT ANSWERS)

1.	C	11.	B
2.	C	12.	C
3.	D	13.	A
4.	A	14.	A
5.	B	15.	C
6.	D	16.	B
7.	C	17.	C
8.	A	18.	B
9.	D	19.	A
10.	D	20.	B

21. A
22. C
23. B
24. D
25. B

TEST 2

Questions 1-6.

DIRECTIONS: Questions 1 through 6 are to be answered SOLELY on the basis of the following passage.

Inherent in all organized endeavors is the need to resolve the individual differences involved in conflict. Conflict may be either a positive or negative factor since it may lead to creativity, innovation and progress on the one hand, or it may result, on the other hand, in a deterioration or even destruction of the organization. Thus, some forms of conflict are desirable, whereas others are undesirable and ethically wrong.

There are three management strategies which deal with interpersonal conflict. In the *divide-and-rule strategy,* management attempts to maintain control by limiting the conflict to those directly involved and preventing their disagreement from spreading to the larger group. The *suppression-of-differences strategy* entails ignoring conflicts or pretending they are irrelevant. In the *working-through-differences strategy,* management actively attempts to solve or resolve intergroup or interpersonal conflicts. Of the three strategies, only the last directly attacks and has the potential for eliminating the causes of conflict. An essential part of this strategy, however, is its employment by a committed and relatively mature management team.

1. According to the above passage, the *divide-and-rule strategy* for dealing with conflict is the attempt to

    A. involve other people in the conflict
    B. restrict the conflict to those participating in it
    C. divide the conflict into positive and negative factors
    D. divide the conflict into a number of smaller ones

2. The word *conflict* is used in relation to both positive and negative factors in this passage. Which one of the following words is MOST likely to describe the activity which the word *conflict,* in the sense of the passage, implies?

    A. Competition   B. Confusion
    C. Cooperation   D. Aggression

3. According to the above passage, which one of the following characteristics is shared by both the *suppression-of-differences strategy* and the *divide-and-rule strategy*?

    A. Pretending that conflicts are irrelevant
    B. Preventing conflicts from spreading to the group situation
    C. Failure to directly attack the causes of conflict
    D. Actively attempting to resolve interpersonal conflict

4. According to the above passage, the successful resolution of interpersonal conflict requires

    A. allowing the group to mediate conflicts between two individuals
    B. division of the conflict into positive and negative factors
    C. involvement of a committed, mature management team
    D. ignoring minor conflicts until they threaten the organization

5. Which can be MOST reasonably inferred from the above passage? Conflict between two individuals is LEAST likely to continue when management uses

   A. the *working-through differences strategy*
   B. the *suppression-of differences strategy*
   C. the *divide-and-rule strategy*
   D. a combination of all three strategies

6. According to the above passage, a DESIRABLE result of conflict in an organization is when conflict

   A. exposes production problems in the organization
   B. can be easily ignored by management
   C. results in advancement of more efficient managers
   D. leads to development of new methods

Questions 7-13.

DIRECTIONS: Questions 7 through 13 are to be answered SOLELY on the basis of the passage below.

Modern management places great emphasis on the concept of communication. The communication process consists of the steps through which an idea or concept passes from its inception by one person, the sender, until it is acted upon by another person, the receiver. Through an understanding of these steps and some of the possible barriers that may occur, more effective communication may be achieved. The first step in the communication process is ideation by the sender. This is the formation of the intended content of the message he wants to transmit. In the next step, encoding, the sender organizes his ideas into a series of symbols designed to communicate his message to his intended receiver. He selects suitable words or phrases that can be understood by the receiver, and he also selects the appropriate media to be used—for example, memorandum, conference, etc. The third step is transmission of the encoded message through selected channels in the organizational structure. In the fourth step, the receiver enters the process by tuning in to receive the message. If the receiver does not function, however, the message is lost. For example, if the message is oral, the receiver must be a good listener. The fifth step is decoding of the message by the receiver, as for example, by changing words into ideas. At this step, the decoded message may not be the same idea that the sender originally encoded because the sender and receiver have different perceptions regarding the meaning of certain words. Finally, the receiver acts or responds. He may file the information, ask for more information, or take other action. There can be no assurance, however, that communication has taken place unless there is some type of feedback to the sender in the form of an acknowledgement that the message was received.

7. According to the above passage, *ideation* is the process by which the

   A. sender develops the intended content of the message
   B. sender organizes his ideas into a series of symbols
   C. receiver tunes in to receive the message
   D. receiver decodes the message

8. In the last sentence of the passage, the word *feedback* refers to the process by which the sender is assured that the

   A. receiver filed the information
   B. receiver's perception is the same as his own
   C. message was received
   D. message was properly interpreted

9. Which one of the following BEST shows the order of the steps in the communication process as described in the passage?

   A. 1 - ideation   2 - encoding
      3 - decoding   4 - transmission
      5 - receiving   6 - action
      7 - feedback to the sender

   B. 1 - ideation   2 - encoding
      3 - transmission 4 - decoding
      5 - receiving   6 - action
      7 - feedback to the sender

   C. 1 - ideation   2 - decoding
      3 - transmission 4 - receiving
      5 - encoding   6 - action
      7 - feedback to the sender

   D. 1 - ideation   2 - encoding
      3 - transmission 4 - receiving
      5 - decoding   6 - action
      7 - feedback to the sender

10. Which one of the following BEST expresses the main theme of the passage?

    A. Different individuals have the same perceptions regarding the meaning of words.
    B. An understanding of the steps in the communication process may achieve better communication.
    C. Receivers play a passive role in the communication process.
    D. Senders should not communicate with receivers who transmit feedback.

11. The above passage implies that a receiver does NOT function properly when he

    A. transmits feedback   B. files the information
    C. is a poor listener   D. asks for more information

12. Which one of the following, according to the above passage, is included in the SECOND step of the communication process?

    A. Selecting the appropriate media to be used in transmission
    B. Formulation of the intended content of the message
    C. Using appropriate media to respond to the receiver's feedback
    D. Transmitting the message through selected channels in the organization

13. The above passage implies that the *decoding process* is MOST NEARLY the reverse of the _____ process.

    A. transmission   B. receiving
    C. feedback   D. encoding

Questions 14-19.

DIRECTIONS: Questions 14 through 19 are to be answered SOLELY on the basis of the following passage.

It is often said that no system will work if the people who carry it out do not want it to work. In too many cases, a departmental reorganization that seemed technically sound and economically practical has proved to be a failure because the planners neglected to take the human factor into account. The truth is that employees are likely to feel threatened when they learn that a major change is in the wind. It does not matter whether or not the change actually poses a threat to an employee; the fact that he believes it does or fears it might is enough to make him feel insecure. Among the dangers he fears, the foremost is the possibility that his job may cease to exist and that he may be laid off or shunted into a less skilled position at lower pay. Even if he knows that his own job category is secure, however, he is likely to fear losing some of the important intangible advantages of his present position—for instance, he may fear that he will be separated from his present companions and thrust in with a group of strangers, or that he will find himself in a lower position on the organizational ladder if a new position is created above his.

It is important that management recognize these natural fears and take them into account in planning any kind of major change. While there is no cut-and-dried formula for preventing employee resistance, there are several steps that can be taken to reduce employees' fears and gain their cooperation. First, unwarranted fears can be dispelled if employees are kept informed of the planning from the start and if they know exactly what to expect. Next, assurance on matters such as retraining, transfers, and placement help should be given as soon as it is clear what direction the reorganization will take. Finally, employees' participation in the planning should be actively sought. There is a great psychological difference between feeling that a change is being forced upon one from the outside, and feeling that one is an insider who is helping to bring about a change.

14. According to the above passage, employees who are not in real danger of losing their jobs because of a proposed reorganization

   A. will be eager to assist in the reorganization
   B. will pay little attention to the reorganization
   C. should not be taken into account in planning the reorganization
   D. are nonetheless likely to feel threatened by the reorganization

15. The passage mentions the *intangible advantages* of a position.
Which of the following BEST describes the kind of advantages alluded to in the passage?

   A. Benefits such as paid holidays and vacations
   B. Satisfaction of human needs for things like friendship and status
   C. Qualities such as leadership and responsibility
   D. A work environment that meets satisfactory standards of health and safety

16. According to the passage, an employee's fear that a reorganization may separate him from his present companions is a (n)

   A. childish and immature reaction to change
   B. unrealistic feeling since this is not going to happen

C. possible reaction that the planners should be aware of
D. incentive to employees to participate in the planning

17. On the basis of the above passage, it would be DESIRABLE, when planning a departmental reorganization, to

   A. be governed by employee feelings and attitudes
   B. give some employees lower positions
   C. keep employees informed
   D. lay off those who are less skilled

18. What does the passage say can be done to help gain employees' cooperation in a reorganization?

   A. Making sure that the change is technically sound, that it is economically practical, and that the human factor is taken into account
   B. Keeping employees fully informed, offering help in fitting them into new positions, and seeking their participation in the planning
   C. Assuring employees that they will not be laid off, that they will not be reassigned to a group of strangers, and that no new positions will be created on the organization ladder
   D. Reducing employees' fears, arranging a retraining program, and providing for transfers

19. Which of the following suggested titles would be MOST appropriate for this passage?

   A. PLANNING A DEPARTMENTAL REORGANIZATION
   B. WHY EMPLOYEES ARE AFRAID
   C. LOOKING AHEAD TO THE FUTURE
   D. PLANNING FOR CHANGE: THE HUMAN FACTOR

Questions 20-22.

DIRECTIONS: Questions 20 through 22 are to be answered SOLELY on the basis of the following passage.

The achievement of good human relations is essential if a business office is to produce at top efficiency and is to be a pleasant place in which to work. All office workers plan an important role in handling problems in human relations. They should, therefore, strive to acquire the understanding, tactfulness, and awareness necessary to deal effectively with actual office situations involving co-workers on all levels. Only in this way can they truly become responsible, interested, cooperative, and helpful members of the staff.

20. The selection implies that the MOST important value of good human relations in an office is to develop

   A. efficiency   B. cooperativeness
   C. tact   D. pleasantness and efficiency

21. Office workers should acquire understanding in dealing with

   A. co-workers   B. subordinates
   C. superiors   D. all members of the staff

22. The selection indicates that a highly competent secretary who is also very argumentative is meeting office requirements   22._____

    A. wholly
    B. partly
    C. slightly
    D. not at all

Questions 23-25.

DIRECTIONS: Questions 23 through 25 are to be answered SOLELY on the basis of the following passage.

It is common knowledge that ability to do a particular job and performance on the job do not always go hand in hand. Persons with great potential abilities sometimes fall down on the job because of laziness or lack of interest in the job, while persons with mediocre talents have often achieved excellent results through their industry and their loyalty to the interests of their employers. It is clear; therefore, that in a balanced personnel program, measures of employee ability need to be supplemented by measures of employee performance, for the final test of any employee is his performance on the job.

23. The MOST accurate of the following statements, on the basis of the above paragraph, is that   23._____

    A. employees who lack ability are usually not industrious
    B. an employee's attitudes are more important than his abilities
    C. mediocre employees who are interested in their work are preferable to employees who possess great ability
    D. superior capacity for performance should be supplemented with proper attitudes

24. On the basis of the above paragraph, the employee of most value to his employer is NOT necessarily the one who   24._____

    A. best understands the significance of his duties
    B. achieves excellent results
    C. possesses the greatest talents
    D. produces the greatest amount of work

25. According to the above paragraph, an employee's efficiency is BEST determined by an   25._____

    A. appraisal of his interest in his work
    B. evaluation of the work performed by him
    C. appraisal of his loyalty to his employer
    D. evaluation of his potential ability to perform his work

KEY (CORRECT ANSWERS)

1. B
2. A
3. C
4. C
5. A

6. D
7. A
8. C
9. D
10. B

11. C
12. A
13. D
14. D
15. B

16. C
17. C
18. B
19. D
20. D

21. D
22. B
23. D
24. C
25. B

TEST 3

Questions 1-8.

DIRECTIONS: Questions 1 through 8 are to be answered SOLELY on the basis of the following information and directions.

Assume that you are a clerk in a city agency. Your supervisor has asked you to classify each of the accidents that happened to employees in the agency into the following five categories:

- A. An accident that occurred in the period from January through June, between 9 A.M. and 12 Noon, that was the result of carelessness on the part of the injured employee, that caused the employee to lose less than seven working hours, that happened to an employee who was 40 years of age or over, and who was employed in the agency for less than three years;

- B. An accident that occurred in the period from July through December, after 1 P.M., that was the result of unsafe conditions, that caused the injured employee to lose less than seven working hours, that happened to an employee who was 40 years of age or over, and who was employed in the agency for three years or more;

- C. An accident that occurred in the period from January through June, after 1 P.M., that was the result of carelessness on the part of the injured employee, that caused the injured employee to lose seven or more working hours, that happened to an employee who was less than 40 years old, and who was employed in the agency for three years or more;

- D. An accident that occurred in the period from July through December, between 9 A.M. and 12 Noon, that was the result of unsafe conditions, that caused the injured employee to lose seven or more working hours, that happened to an employee who was less than 40 years old, and who was employed in the agency for less than three years;

- E. Accidents that cannot be classified in any of the foregoing groups. NOTE: In classifying these accidents, an employee's age and length of service are computed as of the date of accident. In all cases, it is to be assumed that each employee has been employed continuously in city service, and that each employee works seven hours a day, from 9 A.M. to 5 P.M., with lunch from 12 Noon to 1 P.M. In each question, consider only the information which will assist you in classifying the accident. Any information which is of no assistance in classifying an accident should not be considered.

1. The unsafe condition of the stairs in the building caused Miss Perkins to have an accident on October 14, 2003 at 4 P.M. When she returned to work the following day at 1 P.M., Miss Perkins said that the accident was the first one that had occurred to her in her ten years of employment with the agency. She was born on April 27, 1962.   1._____

2. On the day after she completed her six-month probationary period of employment with the agency, Miss Green, who had been considered a careful worker by her supervisor, injured her left foot in an accident caused by her own carelessness. She went home immediately after the accident, which occurred at 10 A.M., March 19, 2004, but returned to work at the regular time on the following morning. Miss Green was born July 12, 1963 in New York City.   2._____

3. The unsafe condition of a duplicating machine caused Mr. Martin to injure himself in an accident on September 8, 2006 at 2 P.M. As a result of the accident, he was unable to work the remainder of the day, but returned to his office ready for work on the following morning. Mr. Martin, who has been working for the agency since April 1, 2003, was born in St. Louis on February 1, 1968.

3.___

4. Mr. Smith was hospitalized for two weeks because of a back injury resulted from an accident on the morning of November 16, 2006. Investigation of the accident revealed that it was caused by the unsafe condition of the floor on which Mr. Smith had been walking. Mr. Smith, who is an accountant, has been anemployee of the agency since March 1, 2004, and was born in Ohio on June 10, 1968.

4.___

5. Mr. Allen cut his right hand because he was careless in operating a multilith machine. Mr. Allen, who was 33 years old when the accident took place, has been employed by the agency since August 17, 1992. The accident, which occurred on January 26, 2006, at 2 P.M., caused Mr. Allen to be absent from work for the rest of the day. He was able to return to work the next morning.

5.___

6. Mr. Rand, who is a college graduate, was born on December, 28, 1967, and has been working for the agency since January 7, 2002. On Monday, April 25, 2005, at 2 P.M., his carelessness in operating a duplicating machine caused him to have an accident and to be sent home from work immediately. Fortunately, he was able to return to work at his regular time on the following Wednesday.

6.___

7. Because he was careless in running down a flight of stairs, Mr. Brown fell, bruising his right hand. Although the accident occurred shortly after he arrived for work on the morning of May 22, 2006, he was unable to resume work until 3 P.M. that day. Mr. Brown was born on August 15, 1955, and began working for the agency on September 12, 2003, as a clerk, at a salary of $22,750 per annum.

7.___

8. On December 5, 2005, four weeks after he had begun working for the agency, the unsafe condition of an automatic stapling machine caused Mr. Thomas to injure himself in an accident. Mr. Thomas, who was born on May 19, 1975, lost three working days because of the accident, which occurred at 11:45 A.M.

8.___

Questions 9-10.

DIRECTIONS: Questions 9 and 10 are to be answered SOLELY on the basis of the following paragraph.

An impending reorganization within an agency will mean loss by transfer of several professional staff members from the personnel division. The division chief is asked to designate the persons to be transferred. After reviewing the implications of this reduction of staff with his assistant, the division chief discusses the matter at a staff meeting. He adopts the recommendations of several staff members to have volunteers make up the required reduction.

9. The decision to permit personnel to volunteer for transfer is

   A. *poor;* it is not likely that the members of a division are of equal value to the division chief
   B. *good;* dissatisfied members will probably be more productive elsewhere
   C. *poor;* the division chief has abdicated his responsibility to carry out the order given to him
   D. *good;* morale among remaining staff is likely to improve in a more cohesive framework

10. Suppose that one of the volunteers is a recently appointed employee who has completed his probationary period acceptably, but whose attitude toward division operations and agency administration tends to be rather negative and sometimes even abrasive. Because of his lack of commitment to the division, his transfer is recommended. If the transfer is approved, the division chief should, prior to the transfer,

    A. discuss with the staff the importance of commitment to the work of the agency and its relationship with job satisfaction
    B. refrain from any discussion of attitude with the employee
    C. discuss with the employee his concern about the employee's attitude
    D. avoid mention of attitude in the evaluation appraisal prepared for the receiving division chief

Questions 11-16.

DIRECTIONS: Questions 11 through 16 are to be answered SOLELY on the basis of the following paragraph.

Methods of administration of office activities, much of which consists of providing information and *know-how* needed to coordinate both activities within that particular office and other offices, have been among the last to come under the spotlight of management analysis. Progress has been rapid during the past decade, however, and is now accelerating at such a pace that an *information revolution* in office management appears to be in the making. Although triggered by technological breakthroughs in electronic computers and other giant steps in mechanization, this information revolution must be attributed to underlying forces, such as the increased complexity of both governmental and private enterprise, and ever-keener competition. Size, diversification, specialization of function, and decentralization are among the forces which make coordination of activities both more imperative and more difficult. Increased competition, both domestic and international, leaves little margin for error in managerial decisions. Several developments during recent years indicate an evolving pattern. In 1960, the American Management Association expanded the scope of its activities and changed the name of its Office Management Division to Administrative Services Division. Also in 1960, the magazine *Office Management* merged with the magazine *American Business,* and this new publication was named *Administrative Management.*

11. A REASONABLE inference that can be made from the information in the above paragraph is that an important role of the office manager today is to

    A. work toward specialization of functions performed by his subordinates
    B. inform and train subordinates regarding any new developments in computer technology and mechanization
    C. assist the professional management analysts with the management analysis work in the organization
    D. supply information that can be used to help coordinate and manage the other activities of the organization

12. An IMPORTANT reason for the *information revolution* that has been taking place in office management is the

    A. advance made in management analysis in the past decade
    B. technological breakthrough in electronic computers and mechanization
    C. more competitive and complicated nature of private business and government
    D. increased efficiency of office management techniques in the past ten years

13. According to the above paragraph, specialization of function in an organization is MOST likely to result in

    A. the elimination of errors in managerial decisions
    B. greater need to coordinate activities
    C. more competition with other organizations, both domestic and international
    D. a need for office managers with greater flexibility

14. The word *evolving,* as used in the third from last sentence in the above paragraph, means MOST NEARLY

    A. developing by gradual changes
    B. passing on to others
    C. occurring periodically
    D. breaking up into separate, constituent parts

15. Of the following, the MOST reasonable implication of the changes in names mentioned in the last part of the above paragraph is that these groups are attempting to

    A. professionalize the field of office management and the title of Office Manager
    B. combine two publications into one because of the increased costs of labor and materials
    C. adjust to the fact that the field of office management is broadening
    D. appeal to the top managerial people rather than the office management people in business and government

16. According to the above paragraph, intense competition among domestic and international enterprises makes it MOST important for an organization's managerial staff to

    A. coordinate and administer office activities with other activities in the organization
    B. make as few errors in decision-making as possible
    C. concentrate on decentralization and reduction of size of the individual divisions of the organization
    D. restrict decision-making only to top management officials

Questions 17-21.

DIRECTIONS: Questions 17 through 21 are to be answered SOLELY on the basis of the following passage.

For some office workers, it is useful to be familiar with the four main classes of domestic mail; for others, it is essential. Each class has a different rate of postage, and some have requirements concerning wrapping, sealing, or special information to be placed on the package. First class mail, the class which may not be opened for postal inspection, includes letters, postcards, business reply cards, and other kinds of written matter. There are different rates for some of the kinds of cards which can be sent by first class mail. The maximum weight for an item sent by first class mail is 70 pounds. An item which is not letter size should be marked *First Class* on all sides. Although office workers most often come into contact with first class mail, they may find it helpful to know something about the other classes. Second class mail is generally used for mailing newspapers and magazines. Publishers of these articles must meet certain U.S. Postal Service requirements in order to obtain a permit to use second class mailing rates. Third class mail, which must weigh less than 1 pound, includes printed materials and merchandise parcels. There are two rate structures for this class - a single piece rate and a bulk rate. Fourth class mail, also known as parcel post, includes packages weighing from one to 40 pounds. For more information about these classes of mail and the actual mailing rates, contact your local post office.

17. According to this passage, first class mail is the *only* class which   17.____

    A. has a limit on the maximum weight of an item
    B. has different rates for items within the class
    C. may not be opened for postal inspection
    D. should be used by office workers

18. According to this passage, the one of the following items which may CORRECTLY be sent by fourth class mail is a   18.____

    A. magazine weighing one-half pound
    B. package weighing one-half pound
    C. package weighing two pounds
    D. postcard

19. According to this passage, there are different postage rates for   19.____

    A. a newspaper sent by second class mail and a magazine sent by second class mail
    B. each of the classes of mail
    C. each pound of fourth class mail
    D. printed material sent by third class mail and merchandise parcels sent by third class mail

20. In order to send a newspaper by second class mail, a publisher MUST   20.____

    A. have met certain postal requirements and obtained a permit
    B. indicate whether he wants to use the single piece or the bulk rate
    C. make certain that the newspaper weighs less than one pound
    D. mark the newspaper *Second Class* on the top and bottom of the wrapper

21. Of the following types of information, the one which is NOT mentioned in the passage is the 21.___

    A. class of mail to which parcel post belongs
    B. kinds of items which can be sent by each class of mail
    C. maximum weight for an item sent by fourth class mail
    D. postage rate for each of the four classes of mail

Questions 22-25.

DIRECTIONS: Questions 22 through 25 are to be answered SOLELY on the basis of the following paragraph.

A standard comprises characteristics attached to an aspect of a process or product by which it can be evaluated. Standardization is the development and adoption of standards. When they are formulated, standards are not usually the product of a single person, but represent the thoughts and ideas of a group, leavened with the knowledge and information which are currently available. Standards which do not meet certain basic requirements become a hindrance rather than an aid to progress. Standards must not only be correct, accurate, and precise in requiring no more and no less than what is needed for satisfactory results, but they must also be workable in the sense that their usefulness is not nullified by external conditions. Standards should also be acceptable to the people who use them. If they are not acceptable, they cannot be considered to be satisfactory, although they may possess all the other essential characteristics.

22. According to the above paragraph, a processing standard that requires the use of materials that cannot be procured is MOST likely to be 22.___

    A. incomplete   B. unworkable
    C. inaccurate   D. unacceptable

23. According to the above paragraph, the construction of standards to which the performance of job duties should conform is MOST often 23.___

    A. the work of the people responsible for seeing that the duties are properly performed
    B. accomplished by the person who is best informed about the functions involved
    C. the responsibility of the people who are to apply them
    D. attributable to the efforts of various informed persons

24. According to the above paragraph, when standards call for finer tolerances than those essential to the conduct of successful production operations, the effect of the standards on the improvement of production operations is 24.___

    A. negative   B. negligible
    C. nullified   D. beneficial

25. The one of the following which is the MOST suitable title for the above paragraph is 25.___

    A. THE EVALUATION OF FORMULATED STANDARDS
    B. THE ATTRIBUTES OF SATISFACTORY STANDARDS
    C. THE ADOPTION OF ACCEPTABLE STANDARDS
    D. THE USE OF PROCESS OR PRODUCT STANDARDS

KEY (CORRECT ANSWERS)

1.	B	11.	D
2.	A	12.	C
3.	E	13.	B
4.	D	14.	A
5.	E	15.	C
6.	C	16.	B
7.	A	17.	C
8.	D	18.	C
9.	A	19.	B
10.	C	20.	A

21. D
22. C
23. D
24. A
25. B

PREPARING WRITTEN MATERIAL

PARAGRAPH REARRANGEMENT
COMMENTARY

The sentences that follow are in scrambled order. You are to rearrange them in proper order and indicate the letter choice containing the correct answer at the space at the right.

Each group of sentences in this section is actually a paragraph presented in scrambled order. Each sentence in the group has a place in that paragraph; no sentence is to be left out. You are to read each group of sentences and decide upon the best order in which to put the sentences so as to form a well-organized paragraph.

The questions in this section measure the ability to solve a problem when all the facts relevant to its solution are not given.

More specifically, certain positions of responsibility and authority require the employee to discover connection between events sometimes, apparently, unrelated. In order to do this, the employee will find it necessary to correctly infer that unspecified events have probably occurred or are likely to occur. This ability becomes especially important when action must be taken on incomplete information.

Accordingly, these questions require competitors to choose among several suggested alternatives, each of which presents a different sequential arrangement of the events. Competitors must choose the MOST logical of the suggested sequences.

In order to do so, they may be required to draw on general knowledge to infer missing concepts or events that are essential to sequencing the given events. Competitors should be careful to infer only what is essential to the sequence. The plausibility of the wrong alternatives will always require the inclusion of unlikely events or of additional chains of events which are NOT essential to sequencing the given events.

It's very important to remember that you are looking for the best of the four possible choices, and that the best choice of all may not even be one of the answers you're given to choose from.

There is no one right way to solve these problems. Many people have found it helpful to first write out the order of the sentences, as they would have arranged them, on their scrap paper before looking at the possible answers. If their optimum answer is there, this can save them some time. If it isn't, this method can still give insight into solving the problem. Others find it most helpful to just go through each of the possible choices, contrasting each as they go along. You should use whatever method feels comfortable and works for you.

While most of these types of questions are not that difficult, we've added a higher percentage of the difficult type, just to give you more practice. Usually there are only one or two questions on this section that contain such subtle distinctions that you're unable to answer confidently. And you then may find yourself stuck deciding between two possible choices, neither of which you're sure about.

EXAMINATION SECTION

TEST 1

DIRECTIONS: The following groups of sentences need to be arranged in an order that makes sense. Select the letter preceding the sequence that represents the BEST sentence order. *PRINT THE LETTER OF THE CORRECT ANSWER IN THE SPACE AT THE RIGHT.*

1. I. The keyboard was purposely designed to be a little awkward to slow typists down.
    II. The arrangement of letters on the keyboard of a typewriter was not designed for the convenience of the typist.
    III. Fortunately, no one is suggesting that a new keyboard be designed right away.
    IV. If one were, we would have to learn to type all over again.
    V. The reason was that the early machines were slower than the typists and would jam easily.
    The CORRECT answer is:
    A. I, III, IV, II, V
    B. II, V, I, IV, III
    C. V, I, II, III, IV
    D. II, I, V, III, IV

    1.____

2. I. The majority of the new service jobs are part-time or low-paying.
    II. According to the U.S. Bureau of Labor Statistics, jobs in the service sector constitute 72% of all jobs in this country.
    III. If more and more workers receive less and less money, who will buy the goods and services needed to keep the economy going?
    IV. The service sector is by far the fastest growing part of the United States economy.
    V. Some economists look upon this trend with great concern.
    The CORRECT answer is:
    A. II, IV, I, V, III
    B. II, III, IV, I, V
    C. V, IV, II, III, I
    D. III, I, II, IV, V

    2.____

3. I. They can also affect one's endurance.
    II. This can stabilize blood sugar levels, and ensure that the brain is receiving a steady, constant, supply of glucose, so that one is *hitting on all cylinders* while taking the test.
    III. By food, we mean real food, not junk food or unhealthy snacks.
    IV. For this reason, it is important not to skip a meal, and to bring food with you to the exam.
    V. One's blood sugar levels can affect how clearly one is able to think and concentrate during an exam.
    The CORRECT answer is:
    A. V, IV, II, III, I
    B. V, II, I, IV, III
    C. V, I, IV, III, II
    D. V, IV, I, III, II

    3.____

4.
I. Those who are the embodiment of desire are absorbed in material quests, and those who are the embodiment of feeling are warriors who value power more than possession.
II. These qualities are in everyone, but in different degrees.
III. But those who value understanding yearn not for goods or victory, but for knowledge.
IV. According to Plato, human behavior flows from three main sources: desire, emotion, and knowledge.
V. In the perfect state, the industrial forces would produce but not rule, the military would protect but not rule, and the forces of knowledge, the philosopher kings, would reign.
The CORRECT answer is:
A. IV, V, I, II, III
B. V, I, II, III, IV
C. IV, III, II, I, V
D. IV, II, I, III, V

4.____

5.
I. Of the more than 26,000 tons of garbage produced daily in New York City, 12,000 tons arrive daily at Fresh Kills.
II. In a month, enough garbage accumulates there to fill the Empire State Building.
III. In 1937, the Supreme Court halted the practice of dumping the trash of New York City into the sea.
IV. Although the garbage is compacted, in a few years the mounds of garbage at Fresh Kills will be the highest points south of Maine's Mount Desert Island on the Eastern Seaboard.
V. Instead, tugboats now pull barges of much of the trash to Staten Island and the largest landfill in the world, Fresh Kills.
The CORRECT answer is:
A. III, V, IV, I, II
B. III, V, II, IV, I
C. III, V, I, II, IV
D. III, II, V, IV, I

5.____

6.
I. Communists rank equality very high, but freedom very low.
II. Unlike communists, conservatives place a high value on freedom and a very low value on equality.
III. A recent study demonstrated that one way to classify people's political beliefs is to look at the importance placed on two words: freedom and equality.
IV. Thus, by demonstrating how members of these groups feel about the two words, the study has proved to be useful for political analysts in several European countries.
V. According to the study, socialists and liberals rank both freedom and equality very high, while fascists rate both very low.
The CORRECT answer is:
A. III, V, I, II, IV
B. V, IV, III, I, II
C. III, V, IV, II, I
D. III, I, II, IV, V

6.____

7. I. "Can there be anything more amazing than this?"
    II. If the riddle is successfully answered, his dead brothers will be brought back to life.
    III. "Even though man sees those around him dying every day," says Dharmaraj, "he still believes and acts as if he were immortal."
    IV. "What is the cause of ceaseless wonder?" asks the Lord of the Lake.
    V. In the ancient epic, The Mahabharata, a riddle is asked of one of the Pandava brothers.
    The CORRECT answer is:
    A. V, II, I, IV, III
    B. V, IV, III, I, II
    C. V, II, IV, III, I
    D. V, II, IV, I, III

8. I. On the contrary, the two main theories—the cooperative (neoclassical) theory and the radical (labor theory)—clearly rest on very different assumptions, which have very different ethical overtones.
    II. The distribution of income is the primary factor in determining the relative levels of material well-being that different groups or individuals attain.
    III. Of all issues in economics, the distribution of income is one of the most controversial.
    IV. The neoclassical theory tends to support the existing income distribution (or minor changes), while the labor theory ends to support substantial changes in the way income is distributed.
    V. The intensity of the controversy reflects the fact that different economic theories are not purely neutral, *detached* theories with no ethical or moral implications.
    The CORRECT answer is:
    A. II, I, V, IV, III
    B. III, II, V, I, IV
    C. III, V, II, I, IV
    D. III, V, IV, I, II

9. I. The pool acts as a broker and ensures that the cheapest power gets used first.
    II. Every six seconds, the pool's computer monitors all of the generating stations in the state and decides which to ask for more power and which to cut back.
    III. The buying and selling of electrical power is handled by the New York Power Pool in Guilderland, New York.
    IV. This is to the advantage of both the buying and selling utilities.
    V. The pool began operation in 1970, and consists of the state's eight electric utilities.
    The CORRECT answer is:
    A. V, I, II, III, IV
    B. IV, II, I, III, V
    C. III, V, I, IV, II
    D. V, III, IV, II, I

10. I. Modern English is much simpler grammatically than Old English.
    II. Finnish grammar is very complicated; there are some fifteen cases, for example.
    III. Chinese, a very old language, may seem to be the exception, but it is the great number of characters/words that must be mastered that makes it so difficult to learn, not its grammar.
    IV. The newest literary language—that is, written as well as spoken—is Finish, whose literary roots go back only to about the middle of the nineteenth century.
    V. Contrary to popular belief, the longer a language is been in use the simpler its grammar—not the reverse.
    The CORRECT answer is:
    A. IV, I, II, III, V
    B. V, I, IV, II, III
    C. I, II, IV, III, V
    D. IV, II, III, I, V

10.____

KEY (CORRECT ANSWERS)

1. D   6. A
2. A   7. C
3. C   8. B
4. D   9. C
5. C   10. B

TEST 2

DIRECTIONS: This type of question tests your ability to recognize accurate paraphrasing, well-constructed paragraphs, and appropriate style and tone. It is important that the answer you select contains only the facts or concepts given in the original sentences. It is also important that you be aware of incomplete sentences, inappropriate transitions, unsupported opinions, incorrect usage, and illogical sentence order. Paragraphs that do not include all the necessary facts and concepts, that distort them, or that add new ones are not considered correct.

The format for this section may vary. Sometimes, long paragraphs are given, and emphasis is placed on style and organization. Our first five questions are of this type. Other times, the paragraphs are shorter, and there is less emphasis on style and more emphasis on accurate representation of information. Our second group of five questions are of this nature.

For each of Questions 1 through 10, select the paragraph that BEST expresses the ideas contained in the sentences above it. *PRINT THE LETTER OF THE CORRECT ANSWER IN THE SPACE AT THE RIGHT.*

1.
   I. Listening skills are very important for managers.
   II. Listening skills are not usually emphasized.
   III. Whenever managers are depicted in books, manuals or the media, they are always talking, never listening.
   IV. We'd like you to read the enclosed handout on listening skills and to try to consciously apply them this week.
   V. We guarantee they will improve the quality of your interactions.

   1.____

   A. Unfortunately, listening skills are not usually emphasized for managers. Managers are always depicted as talking, never listening. We'd like you to read the enclosed handout on listening skills. Please try to apply these principles this week. If you do, we guarantee they will improve the quality of your interactions.
   B. The enclosed handout on listening skills will be important improving the quality of your interactions. We guarantee it. All you have to do is take sometime this week to read and to consciously try to apply the principles. Listening skills are very important for manages, but they are not usually emphasized. Whenever managers are depicted in books, manuals or the media, they are always talking, never listening.
   C. Listening well is one of the most important skills a manager can have, yet it's not usually given much attention. Think about any representation of managers in books, manuals, or in the media that you may have seen. They're always talking, never listening. We'd like you to read the enclosed handout on listening skills and consciously try to apply them the rest of the week. We guarantee you will see a difference in the quality of your interactions.

D. Effective listening, one very important tool in the effective manager's arsenal, is usually not emphasized enough. The usual depiction of managers in books, manuals or the media is one in which they are always talking, never listening. We'd like you to read the enclosed handout and consciously try to apply the information contained therein throughout the rest of the week. We feel sure that you will see a marked difference in the quality of your interactions.

2. I. Chekhov wrote three dramatic masterpieces which share certain themes and formats: <u>Uncle Vanya</u>, <u>The Cherry Orchard</u>, and <u>The Three Sisters</u>.
    II. They are primarily concerned with the passage of time and how this erodes human aspirations.
    III. The plays are haunted by the ghosts of the wasted life.
    IV. The characters are concerned with life's lesser problems; however, such as the inability to make decisions, loyalty to the wrong cause, and the inability to be clear.
    V. This results in sweet, almost aching, type of a sadness referred to as Chekhovian.

    A. Chekhov wrote three dramatic masterpieces: <u>Uncle Vanya</u>, <u>The Cherry Orchard</u>, and <u>The Three Sisters</u>. These masterpieces share certain themes and formats: the passage of time, how time erodes human aspirations, and the ghosts of wasted life. Each masterpiece is characterized by a sweet, almost aching, type of sadness that has become known as Chekhovian. The sweetness of this sadness hinges on the fact that it is not the great tragedies of life which are destroying these characters, but their minor flaws: indecisiveness, misplaced loyalty, unclarity.
    B. <u>The Cherry Orchard</u>, <u>Uncle Vanya</u>, and <u>The Three Sisters</u> are three dramatic masterpieces written by Chekhov that use similar formats to explore a common theme. Each is primarily concerned with the way that passing time wears down human aspirations, and each is haunted by the ghosts of the wasted life. The characters are shown struggling futilely with the lesser problems of life: indecisiveness, loyalty to the wrong cause, and the inability to be clear. These struggles create a mood of sweet, almost aching, sadness that has become known as Chekhovian.
    C. Chekhov's dramatic masterpieces are, along with <u>The Cherry Orchard</u>, <u>Uncle Vanya</u>, and <u>The Three Sisters</u>. These plays share certain thematic and formal similarities. They are concerned most of all with the passage of time and the way in which time erodes human aspirations. Each play is haunted by the specter of the wasted life. Chekhov's characters are caught, however, by life's lesser snares: indecisiveness, loyalty to the wrong cause, and unclarity. The characteristic mood is a sweet, almost aching type of sadness that has come to be known as Chekhovian.
    D. A Chekhovian mood is characterized by sweet, almost aching, sadness. The term comes from three dramatic tragedies by Chekhov which revolve around the sadness of a wasted life. The three masterpieces (<u>Uncle Vanya</u>, <u>The Three Sisters</u>, and <u>The Cherry Orchard</u>) share the same

theme and format. The plays are concerned with how the passage of time erodes human aspirations. They are peopled with characters who are struggling with life's lesser problems. These are people who are indecisive, loyal to the wrong causes, or are unable to make themselves clear.

3.
   I. Movie previews have often helped producers decide which parts of movies they should take out or leave in.
   II. The first 1933 preview of King Kong was very helpful to the producers because many people ran screaming from the theater and would not return when four men first attacked by Kong were eaten by giant spiders.
   III. The 1950 premiere of Sunset Boulevard resulted in the filming of an entirely new beginning, and a delay of six months in the film's release.
   IV. In the original opening scene, William Holden was in a morgue talking with thirty-six other "corpses" about the ways some of them had died.
   V. When he began to tell them of his life with Gloria Swanson, the audience found this hilarious, instead of taking the scene seriously.

3.____

   A. Movie previews have often helped producers decide what parts of movies they should leave in or take out. For example, the first preview of King Kong in 1933 was very helpful. In one scene, four men were first attacked by Kong and then eaten by giant spiders. Many members of the audience ran screaming from the theater and would not return. The premiere of the 1950 film Sunset Boulevard was also very helpful. In the original opening scene, William Holden was in a morgue with thirty-six other "corpses," discussing the ways some of them had died. When he began to tell them of his life with Gloria Swanson, the audience found this hilarious. They were supposed to take the scene seriously. The result was a delay of six months in the release of the film while a new beginning was added.

   B. Movie previews have often helped producers decide whether they should change various parts of a movie. After the 1933 preview of King Kong, a scene in which four men who had been attacked by Kong were eaten by giant spiders was taken out as many people ran screaming from the theater and would not return. The 1950 premiere of Sunset Boulevard also led to some changes. In the original opening scene, William Holden was in a morgue talking with thirty-six other "corpses" about the ways some of them had died. When he began to tell them of his life with Gloria Swanson, the audience found this hilarious, instead of taking the scene seriously.

   C. What do Sunset Boulevard and King Kong have in common? Both show the value of using movie previews to test audience reaction. The first 1933 preview of King Kong showed that a scene showing four men being eaten by giant spiders after having been attacked by Kong was too frightening for many people. They ran screaming from the theater and couldn't be coaxed back. The 1950 premiere of Sunset Boulevard was also a scream, but not the kind the producers intended. The movie opens with William Holden lying in a morgue discussing the ways they had died with thirty-six other "corpses." When he began to tell them of his life with Gloria Swanson, the audience couldn't take him seriously. Their laughter caused a six-month delay while the beginning was rewritten.

D. Producers very often use movie previews to decide if changes are needed. The premiere of Sunset Boulevard in 1950 led to a new beginning and a six-month delay in film release. At the beginning, William Holden and thirty-six other "corpses" discuss the ways some of them died. Rather than taking this seriously, the audience thought it was hilarious when he began to tell them of his life with Gloria Swanson. The first 1933 preview of King Kong was very helpful for its producers because one scene so terrified the audience that many of them ran screaming from the theater and would not return. In this particular scene, four men who had first been attacked by Kong were eaten by giant spiders.

4.
I. It is common for supervisors to view employees as "things" to be manipulated. 4.____
II. This approach does not motivate employees, nor does the carrot-and-stick approach because employees often recognize these behaviors and resent them.
III. Supervisors can change these behaviors by using self-inquiry and persistence.
IV. The best managers genuinely respect those they work with, are supportive and helpful, and are interested in working as a team with those they supervise.
V. They disagree with the Golden Rule that says "he or she who has the gold makes the rules."

A. Some managers act as if they think the Golden Rule means "he or she who has the gold makes the rules." They show disrespect to employees by seeing them as "things" to be manipulated. Obviously, this approach does not motivate employees any more than the carrot-and-stick approach motivates them. The employees are smart enough to spot these behaviors and resent them. On the other hand, the managers genuinely respect those they work with, are supportive and helpful, and are interested in working as a team. Self-inquiry and persistence can change even the former type of supervisor into the latter.
B. Many supervisors all into the trap of viewing employees as "things" to be manipulated, or try to motivate them by using a carrot-and-stick approach. These methods do not motivate employees, who often recognize the behaviors and resent them. Supervisors can change these behaviors, however, by using self-inquiry and persistence. The best managers are supportive and helpful, and have genuine respect for those with whom they work. They are interested in working as a team with those they supervise. To them, the Golden Rule is not "he or she who has the gold makes the rules."
C. Some supervisors see employees as "things" to be used or manipulated using a carrot-and-stick technique. These methods don't work. Employees often see through them and resent them. A supervisor who

wants to change may do so. The techniques of self-inquiry and persistence can be used to turn him or her into the type of supervisor who doesn't think the Golden Rule is "he or she who has the gold makes the rules." They may become like the best managers who treat those with whom they work with respect and give them help and support. These are the manager who know how to build a team.

D. Unfortunately, many supervisors act as if their employees are objects whose movements they can position at will. This mistaken belief has the same result as another popular motivational technique—the carrot-and-stick approach. Both attitudes can lead to the same result—resentment from those employees who recognize the behaviors for what they are. Supervisors who recognize these behaviors can change through the use of persistence and the use of self-inquiry. It's important to remember that the best managers respect their employees. They readily give necessary help and support and are interested in working as a team with those they supervise. To these managers, the Golden Rule is not "he or she who has the gold makes the rules."

5.
I. The first half of the nineteenth century produced a group of pessimistic poets—Byron, De Musset, Heine, Pushkin, and Leopardi.
II. It also produced a group of pessimistic composers—Schubert, Chopin, Schumann, and even the later Beethoven.
III. Above all, in philosophy, there was the profoundly pessimistic philosopher, Schopenhauer.
IV. The Revolution was dead, the Bourbons were restored, the feudal barons were reclaiming their land, and progress everywhere was being suppressed, as the great age was over.
V. "I thank God," said Goethe, "that I am not young in so thoroughly finished a world."

5._____

A. "I thank God," said Goethe, "that I am not young in so thoroughly finished a world." The Revolution was dead, the Bourbons were restored, the feudal barons were reclaiming their land, and progress everywhere was being suppressed. The first half of the nineteenth century produced a group of pessimistic poets: Byron, De Musset, Heine, Pushkin, and Leopardi. It also produced pessimistic composers: Schubert, Chopin, Schumann. Although Beethoven came later, he fits into this group, too. Finally and above all, it also produced a profoundly pessimistic philosopher, Schopenhauer. The great age was over.

B. The first half of the nineteenth century produced a group of pessimistic poets: Byron, De Musset, Heine, Pushkin, and Leopardi. It produced a group of pessimistic composers: Schubert, Chopin, Schumann, and even the later Beethoven. Above all, it produced a profoundly pessimistic philosopher, Schopenhauer. For each of these men, the great age was over. The Revolution was dead, and the Bourbons were restored. The feudal barons were reclaiming their land, and progress everywhere was being suppressed.

C. The great age was over. The Revolution was dead—the Bourbons were restored, and the feudal barons were reclaiming their land. Progress everywhere was being suppressed. Out of this climate came a profound pessimism. Poets, like Byron, De Musset, Heine, Pushkin, and Leopardi; composers, like Schubert, Chopin, Schumann, and even the later Beethoven; and above all, a profoundly pessimistic philosopher, Schopenauer. This pessimism which arose in the first half of the nineteenth century is illustrated by these words of Goethe, "I thank God that I am not young in so thoroughly finished a world."

D. The first half of the nineteenth century produced a group of pessimistic poets, Byron, De Musset, Heine, Pushkin, and Leopardi—and a group of pessimistic composers, Schubert, Chopin, Schumann, and the later Beethoven. Above it all, it produced a profoundly pessimistic philosopher, Schopenhauer. The great age was over. The Revolution was dead, the Bourbons were restored, the feudal barons were reclaiming their land, and progress everywhere was being suppressed. "I thank God," said Goethe, "that I am not young in so thoroughly finished a world."

6. I. A new manager sometimes may feel insecure about his or her competence in the new position.
    II. The new manager may then exhibit defensive or arrogant behavior towards those one supervises, or the new manager may direct overly flattering behavior toward one's new supervisor.

    A. Sometimes, a new manager may feel insecure about his or her ability to perform well in this new position. The insecurity may lead him or her to treat others differently. He or she may display arrogant or defensive behavior towards those he or she supervises, or be overly flattering to his or her new supervisor.
    B. A new manager may sometimes feel insecure about his or her ability to perform well in the new position. He or she may then become arrogant, defensive, or overly flattering towards those he or she works with.
    C. There are times when a new manager may be insecure about how well he or she can perform in the new job. The new manager may also behave defensive or act in an arrogant way towards those he or she supervises, or overly flatter his or her boss.
    D. Sometimes a new manager may feel insecure about his or her ability to perform well in the new position. He or she may then display arrogant or defensive behavior towards those they supervise, or become overly flattering towards their supervisors.

7. I. It is possible to eliminate unwanted behavior by bringing it under stimulus control—tying the behavior to a cue, and then never, or rarely, giving the cue.
    II. One trainer successfully used this method to keep an energetic young porpoise from coming out of her tank whenever she felt like it, which was potentially dangerous.
    III. Her trainer taught her to do it for a reward, in response to a hand signal, and then rarely gave the signal.

A. Unwanted behavior can be eliminated by tying the behavior to a cue, and then never, or rarely, giving the cue. This is called stimulus control. One trainer was able to use this method to keep an energetic young porpoise from coming out of her tank by teaching her to come out for a reward in response to a hand signal, and then rarely giving the signal.
B. Stimulus control can be used to eliminate unwanted behavior. In this method, behavior is tied to a cue, and then the cue is rarely, if ever, given. One trainer was able to successfully use stimulus control to keep an energetic young porpoise from coming out of her tank whenever she felt like it—a potentially dangerous practice. She taught the porpoise to come out for a reward when she gave a hand signal, and then rarely gave the signal.
C. It is possible to eliminate behavior that is undesirable by bringing it under stimulus control by tying behavior to a signal, and then rarely giving the signal. One trainer successfully used this method to keep an energetic porpoise from coming out of her tank, a potentially dangerous situation. Her trainer taught the porpoise to do it for a reward, in response to a hand signal, and then would rarely give the signal.
D. By using stimulus control, it is possible to eliminate unwanted behavior by tying the behavior to a cue, and then rarely or never give the cue. One trainer was able to use this method to successfully stop a young porpoise from coming out of her tank whenever she felt like it. To curb this potentially dangerous practice, the porpoise was taught by the trainer to come out of the tank for a reward, in response to a hand signal, and then rarely given the signal.

8.
 I. There is a great deal of concern over the safety of commercial trucks, caused by their greatly increased role in serious accidents since federal deregulation in 1981.
 II. Recently, 60 percent of trucks in New York and Connecticut and 70 percent of trucks in Maryland randomly stopped by state troopers failed safety inspections.
 III. Sixteen states in the United States require no training at all for truck drivers.

8.____

   A. Since federal deregulation in 1981, there has been a great deal of concern over the safety of commercial trucks, and their greatly increased role in serious accidents. Recently, 60 percent of trucks in New York and Connecticut, and 70 percent of trucks in Maryland failed safety inspections. Sixteen states in the United States require no training at all for truck drivers.
   B. There is a great deal of concern over the safety of commercial trucks since federal deregulation in 1981. Their role in serious accidents has greatly increased. Recently, 60 percent of trucks randomly stopped in Connecticut and New York and 70 percent in Maryland failed safety inspections conducted by state troopers. Sixteen states in the United States provide no training at all for truck drivers.
   C. Commercial trucks have a greatly increased role in serious accidents since federal deregulation in 1981. This has led to a great deal of concern.

Recently, 70 percent of trucks in Maryland and 60 percent of trucks in New York and Connecticut failed inspection of those that were randomly stopped by state troopers. Sixteen states in the United States require no training for all truck drivers.

D. Since federal deregulation in 1981, the role that commercial trucks have played in serious accidents has greatly increased, and this has led to a great deal of concern. Recently, 60 percent of trucks in New York and Connecticut, and 70 percent of trucks in Maryland randomly stopped by state troopers failed safety inspections. Sixteen states in the U.S. don't require any training for truck drivers.

9.
I. No matter how much some people have, they still feel unsatisfied and want more, or want to keep what they have forever.
II. One recent television documentary showed several people flying from New York to Paris for a one-day shopping spree to buy platinum earrings, because they were bored.
III. In Brazil, some people were ordering coffins that cost a minimum of $45,000 and are equipping them with deluxe stereos, televisions, and other graveyard necessities.

9.____

A. Some people, despite having a great deal, still feel unsatisfied and want more, or think they can keep what they have forever. One recent documentary on television showed several people enroute from Paris to New York for a one day shopping spree to buy platinum earrings, because they were bored. Some people in Brazil are even ordering coffins equipped with such graveyard necessities as deluxe stereos and televisions. The price of the coffins start at $45,000.
B. No matter how much some people have, they may feel unsatisfied. This leads them to want more, or to want to keep what they have forever. Recently, a television documentary depicting several people flying from New York to Paris for a one day shopping spree to buy platinum earrings. They were bored. Some people in Brazil are ordering coffins that cost at least $45,000 and come equipped with deluxe televisions, stereos and other necessary graveyard items.
C. Some people will be dissatisfied no matter how much they have. They may want more, or they may want to keep what they have forever. One recent television documentary showed several people, motivated by boredom, jetting from New York to Paris for a one-day shopping spree to buy platinum earrings. In Brazil, some people are ordering coffins equipped with deluxe stereos, televisions and other graveyard necessities. The minimum price for these coffins—$45,000.
D. Some people are never satisfied. No matter how much they have they still want more, or think they can keep what they have forever. One television documentary recently showed several people flying from New York to Paris for the day to buy platinum earrings because they were bored. In Brazil, some people are ordering coffins that cost $45,000 and are equipped with deluxe stereos, televisions and other graveyard necessities.

10. I. A television signal or video signal has three parts.
    II. Its parts are the black-and-white portion, the color portion, and the synchronizing (sync) pulses, which keep the picture stable.
    III. Each video source, whether it's a camera or a video-cassette recorder contains its own generator of these synchronizing pulses to accompany the picture that it's sending in order to keep it steady and straight.
    IV. In order to produce a clean recording, a video-cassette recorder must "lock-up" to the sync pulses that are part of the video it is trying to record, and this effort may be very noticeable if the device does not have gunlock.

    10.____

    A. There are three parts to a television or video signal: the black-and-white part, the color part, and the synchronizing (sync) pulses, which keep the picture stable. Whether it's a video-cassette recorder or a camera, each video source contains its own pulse that synchronizes and generates the picture it's sending in order to keep it straight and steady. A video-cassette recorder must "lock up" to the sync pulses that are part of the video it's trying to record. If the device doesn't have gunlock, this effort must be very noticeable.
    B. A video signal or television is comprised of three parts: the black-and-white portion, the color portion, and the sync (synchronizing) pulses, which keep the picture stable. Whether it's a camera or a video-cassette recorder, each video source contains its own generator of these synchronizing pulses. These accompany the picture that it's sending in order to keep it straight and steady. A video-cassette recorder must "lock up" to the sync pulses that are part of the video it is trying to record in order to produce a clean recording. This effort may be very noticeable if the device does not have gunlock.
    C. There are three parts to a television or video signal: the color portion, the black-and-white portion, and the sync (synchronizing pulses). These keep the picture stable. Each video source, whether it's a video-cassette recorder or a camera, generates these synchronizing pulses accompanying the picture it's sending in order to keep it straight and steady. If a clean recording is to be produced, a video-cassette recorder must store the sync pulses that are part of the video it is trying to record. This effort may not be noticeable if the device does not have gunlock.
    D. A television signal or video signal has three parts: the black-and-white portion, the color portion, and the synchronizing (sync) pulses. It's the sync pulses which keep the picture stable, which accompany it and keep it steady and straight. Whether it's a camera or a video-cassette recorder, each video source contains its own generator of these synchronizing pulses. To produce a clean recording, a video-cassette recorder must "lock up" to the sync pulses that are part of the video it is trying to record. If the device does not have gunlock, this effort may be very noticeable.

KEY (CORRECT ANSWERS)

1.	C	6.	A
2.	B	7.	B
3.	A	8.	D
4.	B	9.	C
5.	D	10.	D

PREPARING WRITTEN MATERIAL
EXAMINATION SECTION
TEST 1

DIRECTIONS: The following groups of sentences need to be arranged in an order that makes sense. Select the letter preceding the sequence that represents the BEST sentence order. *PRINT THE LETTER OF THE CORRECT ANSWER IN THE SPACE AT THE RIGHT.*

1. I. A large Naval station on Alameda Island, near Oakland, held many warships in port, and the War Department was worried that if the bridge were to be blown up by the enemy, passage to and from the bay would be hopelessly blocked.
    II. Though many skeptics were opposed to the idea of building such an enormous bridge, the most vocal opposition came from a surprising source: the United States War Department.
    III. The War Department's concerns led to a showdown at San Francisco City Hall between Strauss and the Secretary of War, who demanded to know what would happen if a military enemy blew up the bridge.
    IV. In 1933, by submitting a construction cost estimate of $17 million, an engineer named Joseph Strauss won the contract to build the Golden Gate Bridge of San Francisco, which would then become one of the world's largest bridges.
    V. Strauss quickly ended the debate by explaining that the Golden Gate Bridge was to be a suspension bridge, whose roadway would hang in the air from cables strung between two huge towers, and would immediately sink into three hundred feet of water if it were destroyed.

    The BEST order is:
    A. II, III, I, IV, V   B. I, II, III, V, IV   C. IV, II, I, III, V   D. IV, I, III, V, II

    1.____

2. I. Plastic surgeons have already begun to use virtual reality to map out the complex nerve and tissue structures of a particular patient's face, in order to prepare for delicate surgery.
    II. A virtual reality program responds to these movements by adjusting the images that a person sees on a screen or through goggles, thereby creating an "interactive" world in which a person can see and touch three-dimensional graphic objects.
    III. No more than a computer program that is designed to build and display graphic images, the virtual reality program takes graphic programs a step further by sensing a person's head and body movements.
    IV. The computer technology known as virtual reality, now in its very first stages of development, is already revolutionizing some aspects of contemporary life.
    V. Virtual reality computers are also being used by the space program, most recently to simulate conditions for the astronauts who were launched on a repair mission to the Hubble telescope.

    2.____

The BEST order is:
A. IV, II, I, V, III   B. III, I, V, II, IV   C. IV, III, II, I, V   D. III, I, II, IV, V

3. I. Before you plant anything, the soil in your plant bed should be carefully raked level, a small section at a time, and any clods or rocks that can't be broken up should be removed.
    II. Your plant should be placed in a hole that will position it at the same level it was at the nursery, and a small indentation should be pressed into the soil around the plant in order to hold water near its roots.
    III. Before placing the plant in the soil, lightly separate any roots that may have been matted together in the container, cutting away any thick masses that can't be separated, so that the remaining roots will be able to grow outward.
    IV. After the bed is ready, remove your plant from its container by turning it upside down and tapping or pushing on the bottom —never remove it by pulling on the plant.
    V. When you bring home a small plant in an individual container from the nursery, there are several things to remember while preparing to plant it in your own garden.
    The BEST order is:
    A. V, IV, III, II, I   B. V, II, IV, III, II   C. I, IV, II, III, V   D. I, IV, V, II, III

3.____

4. I. The motte and its tower were usually built first, so that sentries could use it as a lookout to warn the castle workers of any danger that might approach the castle.
    II. Though the moat and palisade offered the bailey a good deal of protection, it was linked to the motte by a set of stairs that led to a retractable drawbridge at the motte's gate, to enable people to evacuate onto the motte in case of an attack.
    III. The motte of these early castles was a fortified hill, sometimes as high as one hundred feet, on which stood a palisade and tower.
    IV. The bailey was a clear, level spot below the motte, also enclosed by a palisade, which in turn was surrounded by a large trench or moat.
    V. The earliest castles built in Europe were not the magnificent stone giants that still tower over much of the European landscape, but simpler wooden constructions called motte-and-bailey castles.
    The BEST order is:
    A. V, III, I, IV, II   B. V, IV, I, II, III   C. I, IV, III, II, V   D. I, III, II, IV, V

4.____

5. I. If an infant is left alone or abandoned for a short while, its immediate response is to cry loudly, accompanying its screams with aggressive flailing of its legs and limbs.
    II. If a child has been abandoned for a longer period of time, it becomes completely still and quiet, as if realizing that now its only chance for survival is to shut its mouth and remain motionless.
    III. Along with their intense fear of the dark, the crying behavior of human infants offers insights into how prehistoric newborn children might have evolved instincts that would prevent them from becoming victims of predators.

5.____

IV. This behavior often surprises people who enter a hospital's maternity ward for the first time and encounter total silence from a roomful of infants.
V. This violent screaming response is quite different from an infant's cries of discomfort or hunger, and seems to serve as either the child's first line of defense against an unwanted intruder, or a desperate attempt to communicate its position to the mother.

The BEST order is:
A. III, II, IV, I, V   B. III, I, V, II, IV   C. I, V, IV, II, III   D. II, IV, I, V, III

6.
I. When two cats meet who are strangers, their first actions and gestures determine who the "dominant" cat will be, at least for the time being.
II. Unlike dogs, cats are typically a solitary animal species who avoid social interaction, but they do display specific social responses to each other upon meeting.
III. This is unlikely, however; before such a point of open hostility is reached, one of the cats will usually take the "submissive" position of crouching down while looking away from the other dat.
IV. If a cat desires dominance or sees the other cat as a threat to its territory, it will stare directly at the intruder with a lowered tail.
V. If the other cat responds with a similar gesture, or with the strong defensive posture of an arched back, laid-back ears and raised tail, a fight or chase is likely if neither cat gives in.

The BEST order is:
A. IV, II, I, V, III   B. I, II, IV, V, III   C. I, IV, V, III, II   D. II, I, IV, V, III

7.
I. A star or planet's gravitational force can best be explained in this way: anything passing through this "dent" in space will veer toward the star or planet as if it were rolling into a hole.
II. Objects that are massive or heavy, such as stars or planets, "sink" into this surface, creating a sort of dent or concavity in the surrounding space.
III. Black holes, the most massive objects known to exist in space, create dents so large and deep that the space surrounding them actually folds in on itself, preventing anything that falls in —even light —from ever escaping again.
IV. The sort of dent a star or planet makes depends on how massive it is; planets generally have weak gravitational pulls, but stars, which are larger and heavier, make a bigger "dent" that will attract more matter.
V. In outer space, the force of gravity works as if the surrounding space is a soft, flat surface.

The BEST order is:
A. III, V, II, I, IV   B. III, IV, I, V, II   C. V, II, I, IV, III   D. I, V, II, IV, III

8.
I. Eventually, the society of Kyoto gave the world one of its first and greatest novels when Japan's most promising writer, Lady Murasaki Shikibu, wrote her chronicle of Kyoto's society, *The Tale of Genji*, which preceded the first European novels by more than 500 years.
II. The society of Kyoto was dedicated to the pleasures of art; the courtiers experimented with new and colorful methods of sculpture, painting, writing, decorative gardening, and even making clothes.

III. Japanese culture began under the powerful authority of Chinese Buddhism, which influenced every aspect of Japanese life from religion to politics and art.
IV. This new, vibrant culture was so sophisticated that all the people in Kyoto's imperial court considered themselves poets, and the line between life and art hardly existed —lovers corresponded entirely through written verses, and even government officials communicated by writing poems to each other.
V. In the eighth century, when the emperor established the town of Kyoto as the capital of the Japanese empire, Japanese society began to develop its own distinctive style.

The BEST order is:
A. V, II, IV, I, III   B. II, I, V, IV, III   C. V, III, IV, I, II   D. III, V, II, IV, I

9. I. Instead of wheels, the HSST uses two sets of magnets, one which sits on the track, and another that is carried by the train; these magnets generate an identical magnetic field which forces the two sets apart.
II. In the last few decades, railway travel has become less popular throughout the world, because it is much slower than travel by airplane, and not much less expensive.
III. The HSST's designers say that the train can take passengers from one town to another as quickly as a jet plane —while consuming less than half the energy.
IV. This repellent effect is strong enough to lift the entire train above the trackway, and the train, literally traveling on air, rockets along at speeds of up to 300 miles per hour.
V. The revolutionary technology of magnetic levitation, currently being tested by Japan's experimental HSST (High Speed Surface Transport), may yet bring passenger trains back from the dead.

The BEST order is:
A. II, V, I, IV, III   B. II, I, IV, III, V   C. V, II, III, I, IV   D. V, I, III, IV, II

10. I. When European countries first began to colonize the African continent, their impression of the African people was of a vast group of loosely organized tribal societies, without any great centralized source of power or wealth.
II. The legend of Timbuktu persisted until the nineteenth century, when a French adventurer visited Timbuktu and found that raids by neighboring tribesmen had made the city a shadow of its former self.
III. In the fifteenth century, when the stories of travelers who had traveled Africa's Sudan region began circulating around Europe, this impression began to change.
IV. In 1470, an Italian merchant named Benedetto Dei traveled to Timbuktu and confirmed these rumors, describing a thriving metropolis where rich and poor people worshipped together in the city's many ornate mosques — there was even a university in Timbuktu, much like its European counterparts, where African scholars pursued their studies in the arts and sciences.

V. The travelers' legends told of an enormous city in the western Sudan, Timbuktu, where the streets were crowded with goods brought by faraway caravans, and where there was a stone palace as large as any in Europe.

The BEST order is:
A. III, V, I, IV, II   B. I, II, IV, III, V   C. I, III, V, IV, II   D. II, I, III, IV, V

11. I. Also, our reference points in sighting the moon make us believe that its size is changing; when the moon is rising through the trees, it seems huge, because our brains unconsciously compare the size of the moon with the size of the trees in the foreground.
II. To most people, the sky itself appears more distant at the horizon than directly overhead, and if the moon's size—which remains constant—is projected from the horizon, the apparent distance of the horizon makes the moon look bigger.
III. Up higher in the sky, the moon is set against tiny stars in the background, which will make the moon seem smaller.
IV. People often wonder why the moon becomes bigger when it approaches the horizon, but most scientists agree that this is a complicated optical illusion, produced by at least three factors.
V. The moon illusion may also be partially explained by a phenomenon that has nothing to do with errors in our perception—light that enters the earth's atmosphere is sometimes refracted, and so the atmosphere may act as a kind of magnifying glass for the moon's image.

The BEST order is:
A. IV, III, V, II, I   B. IV, II, I, III, V   C. V, II, I, III, IV   D. II, I, III, IV, V

11.____

12. I. When the Native Americans were introduced to the horses used by white explorers, they were amazed at their new alternative—here was an animal that was strong and swift, would patiently carry a person or other loads on its back, and they later discovered, was right at home on the plains.
II. Before the arrival of European explorers to North America, the natives of the American plains used large dogs to carry their travois-long lodgepoles loaded with clothing, gear, and food.
III. These horses, it is now known, were not really strangers to North America; the very first horses originated here, on this continent, tens of thousands of years ago, and migrated into Asia across the Bering Land Bridge, a strip of land that used to link our continent with the Eastern world.
IV. At first, the natives knew so little about horses that at least one tribe tried to feed their new animals pieces of dried meat and animal fat, and were surprised when the horses turned their heads away and began to eat the grass of the prairie.
V. The American horse eventually became extinct, but its Asian cousins were reintroduced to the New World when the European explorers brought them to live among the Native Americans.

The BEST order is:
A. II, I, IV, III, V   B. II, IV, I, III, V   C. I, II, IV, III, V   D. I, III, V, II, IV

12.____

13.
I. The dress worn by the dancer is believed to have been adorned in the past by shells which would strike each other as the dancer performed, creating a lovely sound.
II. Today's jingle-dress is decorated with the tin lids of snuff cans, which are rolled into cones and sewn onto the dress,
III. During the jingle-dress dance, the dancer must blend complicated footwork with a series of gentle hos that cause the cones to jingle in rhythm to a drumbeat.
IV. When contemporary Native American tribes meet for a pow-wow, one of the most popular ceremonies to take place is the women's jingle-dress dance.
V. Besides being more readily available than shells, the lids are thought by many dancers to create a softer, more subtle sound.

The BEST order is:
A. II, IV, V, I, III B. IV, II, I, III, V C. II, I, III, V, IV D. IV, I, II, V, III

13._____

14.
I. If a homeowner lives where seasonal climates are extreme, deciduous shade trees—which will drop their leaves in the winter and allow sunlight to pass through the windows—should be planted near the southern exposure in order to keep the house cool during the summer.
II. This trajectory is shorter and lower in the sky than at any other time of year during the winter, when a house most requires heating; the northern-facing parts of a house do not receive any direct sunlight at all.
III. In designing an energy-efficient house, especially in colder climates, it is important to remember that most of the house's windows should face south.
IV. Though the sun always rises in the east and sets in the west, the sun of the northern hemisphere is permanently situated in the southern portion of the sky.
V. The explanation for why so many architects and builders want this "southern exposure" is related to the path of the sun in the sky.

The BEST order is:
A. III, I, V, IV, II B. III, V, IV, II, I C. I, III, IV, II, V D. I, II, V, IV, III

14._____

15.
I. His journeying lasted twenty-four years and took him over an estimated 75,000 miles, a distance that would not be surpassed by anyone other than Magellan—who sailed around the world—for another six hundred years.
II. Perhaps the most far-flung of these lesser-known travelers was Ibn Batuta, an African Moslem who left his birthplace of Tangier in the summer of 1325.
III. Ibn Batuta traveled all over Africa and Asia, from Niger to Peking, and to the islands of Maldive and Indonesia.
IV. However, a few explorers of the Eastern world logged enough miles and adventures to make Marco Polo's voyage look like an evening stroll.
V. In America, the most well-known of the Old World's explorers are usually Europeans such as Marco Polo, the Italian who brought many elements of Chinese culture to the Western world.

The BEST order is:
A. V, IV, II, III, I B. V, IV, III, II, I C. III, II, I, IV, V D. II, III, I, IV, V

15._____

16.
I. In the rainforests of South America, a rare species of frog practices a reproductive method that is entirely different from this standard process.
II. She will eventually carry each of the tadpoles up into the canopy and drop each into its own little pool, where it will be easy to locate and safe from most predators.
III. After fertilization, the female of the species, who lives almost entirely on the forest floor, lays between 2 and 16 eggs among the leaf litter at the base of a tree, and stands watch over these eggs until they hatch.
IV. Most frogs are pond-dwellers who are able to deposit hundreds of eggs in the water and then leave them alone, knowing that enough eggs have been laid to insure the survival of some of their offspring.
V. Once the tadpoles emerge, the female backs in among them, and a tadpole will wriggle onto her back to be carried high into the forest canopy, where the female will deposit it in a little pool of water cupped in the leaf of a plant.
The BEST order is:
A. I, IV, III, II, V B. I, III, V, II, IV C. IV, III, II, V, I D. IV, I, III, V, II

17.
I. Eratosthenes had heard from travelers that at exactly noon on June 21, in the ancient city of Aswan, Egypt, the sun cast no shadow in a well, which meant that the sun must be directly overhead.
II. He knew the sun always cast a shadow in Alexandria, and so he figured that if he could measure the length of an Alexandria shadow at the time when there was no shadow in Aswan, he could calculate the angle of the sun, and therefore the circumference of the earth.
III. The evidence for a round earth was not new in 1492; in fact, Eratosthenes, an Alexandrian geographer who lived nearly sixteen centuries before Columbus's voyage (275-195 B.C.), actually developed a method for calculating the circumference of the earth that is still in use today.
IV. Eratosthenes's method was correct, but his result—28,700 miles—was about 15 percent too high, probably because of the inaccurate ancient methods of keeping time, and because Aswan was not due south of Alexandria, as Eratosthenes had believed.
V. When Christopher Columbus sailed across the Atlantic Ocean for the first time in 1492, there were still some people in the world who ignored scientific evidence and believed that the earth was flat, rather than round.
The BEST order is:
A. I, II, V, III, IV B. V, III, IV, I, II C. V, III, I, II, IV D. III, V, I, II, IV

18.
I. The first name for the child is considered a trial naming, often impersonal and neutral, such as the Ngoni name *Chabwera*, meaning "it has arrived."
II. This sort of name is not due to any parental indifference to the child, but is a kind of silent recognition of Africa's sometimes high infant death rate; most parents ease the pain of losing a child with the belief that it is not really a person until it has been given a final name.
III. In many tribal African societies, families often give two different names to their children, at different periods in time.
IV. After the trial naming period has subsided and it is clear that the child will survive, the parents choose a final name for the child, an act that symbolically completes the act of birth.

V. In fact, some African first-given names are explicitly uncomplimentary, translating as "I am dead" or "I am ugly," in order to avoid the jealousy of ancestral spirits who might wish to take a child that is especially healthy or attractive.

The BEST order is:
A. III, I, II, V, IV   B. III, IV, II, I, V   C. IV, III, I, II, V   D. IV, V, III, I, II

19.
I. Though uncertain of the definite reasons for this behavior, scientists believe the birds digest the clay in order to counteract toxins contained in the seeds of certain fruits that are eaten by macaws.
II. For example, all macaws flock to riverbanks at certain times of the year to eat the clay that is found in river mud.
III. The macaws of South America are not only among the largest and most beautifully colored of the world's flying birds, but they are also one of the smartest.
IV. It is believed that macaws are forced to resort to these toxic fruits during the dry season, when foods are more scarce.
V. The macaw's intelligence has led to intense study by scientists, who have discovered some macaw behaviors that have not yet been explained.

The BEST order is:
A. III, IV, I, II, V   B. III, V, II, I, IV   C. V, II, I, IV, III   D. IV, I, II, III, V

19.____

20.
I. Although Maggie Kuhn has since passed away, the Gray Panthers are still waging a campaign to reinstate the historical view of the elderly as people whose experience allows them to make their greatest contribution in their later years.
II. In 1972, an elderly woman named Maggie Kuhn responded to this sort of treatment by forming a group called the Gray Panthers, an organization of both old and young adults with the common goal of creating change.
III. This attitude is reflected strongly in the way elderly people are treated by our society; many are forced into early retirement, or are placed in rest homes in which they are isolated from their communities.
IV. Unlike most other cultures around the world, Americans tend to look upon old age with a sense of dread and sadness.
V. Kuhn believed that when the elderly are forced to withdraw into lives that lack purpose, society loses one of its greatest resources: people who have a lifetime of experience and wisdom to offer their communities.

The BEST order is:
A. IV, III, II, V, I   B. IV, II, I, III, V   C. II, IV, III, V, I   D. II, I, IV, III, V

20.____

21.
I. The current theory among most anthropologists is that humans evolved from apes who lived in trees near the grasslands of Africa.
II. Still, some anthropologists insist that such an invention was necessary for the survival of early humans, and point to the Kung Bushmen of central Africa as a society in which the sling is still used in this way.
III. Two of these inventions—fire, and weapons such as spears and clubs—were obvious defenses against predators, and there is archaeological evidence to support the theory of their use.

21.____

IV. Once people had evolved enough to leave the safety of trees and walk upright, they needed the protection of several inventions in order to survive.
V. But another invention, a feather or fiber sling that allowed mothers to carry children while leaving their hands free to gather roots or berries, would certainly have decomposed and left behind no trace of itself.

The BEST order is:
A. I, II, III, V, IV   B. IV, I, II, III, V   C. I, IV, III, V, II   D. IV, III, V, II, I

22. I. The person holding the bird should keep it in hot water up to its neck, and the person cleaning should work a mild solution of dishwashing liquid into the bird's plumage, paying close attention to the head and neck.
II. When rinsing the bird, after all the oil has been removed, the running water should be directed against the lay of its feathers, until water begins to bead off the surface of the feathers—a sign that all the detergent has been rinsed out.
III. If you have rescued a sea bird from an oil spill and want to restore it to clean and normal living, you need a large sink, a constant supply of running hot water (a little over 100°F), and regular dishwashing liquid.
IV. This cleaning with detergent solution should be repeated as many times as it takes to remove all traces of oil from the bird's feathers, sometime over a period of several days.
V. But before you begin to clean the bird, you must find a partner because cleaning an oiled bird is a two-person job.

The BEST order is:
A. III, I, II, IV, V   B. III, V, I, IV, II   C. III, I, IV, V, II   D. III, IV, V, I, II

22._____

23. I. The most difficult time of year for the Tsaatang is the spring calving, when the reindeer leave their wintering ground and rush to their accustomed calving place, without stopping by night or by day.
II. Reindeer travel in herds, and though some animals are tamed by the Tsaatang for riding or milking, the herds are allowed to roam free.
III. This journey is hard for the Tsaatang, who carry all their possessions with them, but once it's over it proves worthwhile; the Tsaatang can immediately begin to gather milk from reindeer cows who have given birth.
IV. The Tsaatang, a small tribe who live in the far northwest corner of Mongolia, practice a lifestyle that is completely dependent on the reindeer, their main resource for food, clothing, and transport.
V. The people must follow their yearly migrations, living in portable shelters that resemble Native American tepees.

The BEST order is:
A. I, III, II, V, IV   B. I, IV, II, V, III   C. IV, I, III, V, II   D. IV, II, V, I, III

23._____

24. I. The Romans later improved this system by installing these heated pipe networks throughout walls and ceilings, supplying heat to even the uppermost floors of a building—a system that, to this day, hasn't been much improved.
II. Air-conditioning, the method by which humans control indoor temperatures, was practiced much earlier than most people think.

24._____

III. The earliest heating devices other than open fires were used in 350 B.C. by the ancient Greeks, who directed air that had been heated by underground fires into baked clay pipes that ran under the floor.

IV. Ironically, the first successful cooling system, patented in England in 1831, used fire as its main energy source—fires were lit in the attic of a building, creating an updraft of air that drew cool air into the building through ducts that had underground openings near the river Thames.

V. Cooling buildings was more of a challenge, and wasn't attempted until 1500: a water-based system, designed by Leonardo da Vinci, does not appear to have been successful, since it was never used again.

The BEST order is:

A. III, V, IV, I, II   B. III, I, II, V, IV   C. II, III, I, V, IV   D. IV, II, III, I, V

25. I. Cold, dry air from Canada passes over the Rocky Mountains and sweeps down onto the plains, where it collides with warm, moist air from the waters of the Gulf of Mexico, and when the two air masses meet, the resulting disturbance sometimes forms a violent funnel cloud that strikes the earth and destroys virtually everything in its path.

II. Hurricanes, storms which are generally not this violent and last much longer, are usually given names by meteorologists, but this tradition cannot be applied to tornados, which have a life span measured in minutes and disappear in the same way as they are born—unnamed.

III. A tornado funnel forms rotating columns of air whose speed reaches three hundred miles an hour—a speed that can only be estimated, because no wind-measuring devices in the direct path of a storm have ever survived.

IV. The natural phenomena known as tornados occur primarily over the Midwestern grasslands of the United States.

V. It is here, meteorologists tell us, that conditions for the formation of tornados are sometimes perfect during the spring months.

The BEST order is:

A. II IV, V, I, III   B. II, III, I, V, IV   C. IV, V, I, III, II   D. IV, III, I, V, II

25.____

KEY (CORRECT ANSWERS)

1.	C		11.	B
2.	C		12.	A
3.	B		13.	D
4.	A		14.	B
5.	B		15.	A
6.	D		16.	D
7.	C		17.	C
8.	D		18.	A
9.	A		19.	B
10.	C		20.	A

21. C
22. B
23. D
24. C
25. C

PREPARING WRITTEN MATERIAL
EXAMINATION SECTION
TEST 1

DIRECTIONS: Each of the sentences in this test may be classified under one of the following four categories:
    A. Faulty because of incorrect grammar or word usage
    B. Faulty because of incorrect punctuation
    C. Faulty because of incorrect capitalization or incorrect spelling
    D. Correct

Examine each sentence carefully to determine under which of the above four options it is best classified. Then, in the space to the right, print the capital letter preceding the option which is the BEST of the four suggested above. (Note that each faulty sentence contains but one type of error. Consider a sentence to be correct if it contains none of the types of errors mentioned, even though there may be other correct ways of expressing the same thought.)

1. He sent the notice to the clerk who you hired yesterday.   1.____

2. It must be admitted, however that you were not informed of this change.   2.____

3. Only the employee who have served in this grade for at least two years are eligible for promotion.   3.____

4. The work was divided equally between she and Mary.   4.____

5. He thought that you were not available at that time.   5.____

6. When the messenger returns; please give him this package.   6.____

7. The new secretary prepared, typed, addressed, and delivered, the notices.   7.____

8. Walking into the room, his desk can be seen at the rear.   8.____

9. Although John has worked here longer than She, he produces a smaller amount of work.   9.____

10. She said she could of typed this report yesterday.   10.____

11. Neither one of these procedures are adequate for the efficient performance of this task.   11.____

12. The typewriter is the tool of the typist; the cash register, the tool of the cashier.   12.____

13. "The assignment must be completed as soon as possible" said the supervisor.　　13._____

14. As you know, office handbooks are issued to all new Employees.　　14._____

15. Writing a speech is sometimes easier than to deliver it before an audience.　　15._____

16. Mr. Brown our accountant, will audit the accounts next week.　　16._____

17. Give the assignment to whomever is able to do it most efficiently.　　17._____

18. The supervisor expected either your or I to file these reports.　　18._____

KEY (CORRECT ANSWERS)

1.	A	11.	A
2.	B	12.	C
3.	D	13.	B
4.	A	14.	C
5.	D	15.	A
6.	B	16.	B
7.	B	17.	A
8.	A	18.	A
9.	C		
10.	A		

TEST 2

DIRECTIONS: Each of the sentences in this test may be classified under one of the following four categories:
- A. Faulty because of incorrect grammar or word usage
- B. Faulty because of incorrect punctuation
- C. Faulty because of incorrect capitalization or incorrect spelling
- D. Correct

Examine each sentence carefully to determine under which of the above four options it is best classified. Then, in the space to the right, print the capital letter preceding the option which is the BEST of the four suggested above. (Note that each faulty sentence contains but one type of error. Consider a sentence to be correct if it contains none of the types of errors mentioned, even though there may be other correct ways of expressing the same thought.)

1. The fire apparently started in the storeroom, which is usually locked. 1.____
2. On approaching the victim, two bruises were noticed by this officer. 2.____
3. The officer, who was there examined the report with great care. 3.____
4. Each employee in the office had a seperate desk. 4.____
5. All employees including members of the clerical staff, were invited to the lecture. 5.____
6. The suggested Procedure is similar to the one now in use. 6.____
7. No one was more pleased with the new procedure than the chauffeur. 7.____
8. He tried to persaude her to change the procedure. 8.____
9. The total of the expenses charged to petty cash were high. 9.____
10. An understanding between him and I was finally reached. 10.____

KEY (CORRECT ANSWERS)

1.	D	6.	C
2.	A	7.	D
3.	B	8.	C
4.	C	9.	A
5.	B	10.	A

TEST 3

DIRECTIONS: Each of the sentences in this test may be classified under one of the following four categories:
- A. Faulty because of incorrect grammar or word usage
- B. Faulty because of incorrect punctuation
- C. Faulty because of incorrect capitalization or incorrect spelling
- D. Correct

Examine each sentence carefully to determine under which of the above four options it is best classified. Then, in the space to the right, print the capital letter preceding the option which is the BEST of the four suggested above. (Note that each faulty sentence contains but one type of error. Consider a sentence to be correct if it contains none of the types of errors mentioned, even though there may be other correct ways of expressing the same thought.)

1. They told both he and I that the prisoner had escaped.   1.____

2. Any superior officer, who, disregards the just complaint of his subordinates, is remiss in the performance of his duty.   2.____

3. Only those members of the national organization who resided in the Middle West attended the conference in Chicago.   3.____

4. We told him to give the national organization assignment to whoever was available.   4.____

5. Please do not disappoint and embarass us by not appearing in court.   5.____

6. Although the office's speech proved to be entertaining, the topic was not relevent to the main theme of the conference.   6.____

7. In February all new officers attended a training course in which they were learned in their principal duties and the fundamental operating procedure of the department.   7.____

8. I personally seen inmate Jones threaten inmates Smith and Green with bodily harm if they refused to participate in the plot.   8.____

9. To the layman, who on a chance visit to the prison observes everything functioning smoothly, the maintenance of prison discipline may seem to be a relatively easily realizable objective.   9.____

10. The prisoners in cell block fourty were forbidden to sit on the cell cots during the recreation hour.   10.____

KEY (CORRECT ANSWERS)

1.	A	6.	C
2.	B	7.	A
3.	C	8.	A
4.	D	9.	D
5.	C	10.	C

TEST 4

DIRECTIONS: Each of the sentences in this test may be classified under one of the following four categories:
  A. Faulty because of incorrect grammar or word usage
  B. Faulty because of incorrect punctuation
  C. Faulty because of incorrect capitalization or incorrect spelling
  D. Correct

Examine each sentence carefully to determine under which of the above four options it is best classified. Then, in the space to the right, print the capital letter preceding the option which is the BEST of the four suggested above. (Note that each faulty sentence contains but one type of error. Consider a sentence to be correct if it contains none of the types of errors mentioned, even though there may be other correct ways of expressing the same thought.)

1. I cannot encourage you any.   1._____
2. You always look well in those sort of clothes.   2._____
3. Shall we go to the park?   3._____
4. The man whome he introduced was Mr. Carey.   4._____
5. She saw the letter laying here this morning.   5._____
6. It should rain before the Afternoon is over.   6._____
7. They have already went home.   7._____
8. That Jackson will be elected is evident.   8._____
9. He does not hardly approve of us.   9._____
10. It was he, who won the prize.   10._____

KEY (CORRECT ANSWERS)

1.	A	6.	C
2.	A	7.	A
3.	D	8.	D
4.	C	9.	A
5.	A	10.	B

TEST 5

DIRECTIONS: Each of the sentences in this test may be classified under one of the following four categories:
    A. Faulty because of incorrect grammar or word usage
    B. Faulty because of incorrect punctuation
    C. Faulty because of incorrect capitalization or incorrect spelling
    D. Correct

Examine each sentence carefully to determine under which of the above four options it is best classified. Then, in the space to the right, print the capital letter preceding the option which is the BEST of the four suggested above. (Note that each faulty sentence contains but one type of error. Consider a sentence to be correct if it contains none of the types of errors mentioned, even though there may be other correct ways of expressing the same thought.)

1. Shall we go to the park.   1.____
2. They are, alike, in this particular way.   2.____
3. They gave the poor man sume food when he knocked on the door.   3.____
4. I regret the loss caused by the error.   4.____
5. The students' will have a new teacher.   5.____
6. They sweared to bring out all the facts.   6.____
7. He decided to open a branch store on 33rd street.   7.____
8. His speed is equal and more than that of a racehorse.   8.____
9. He felt very warm on that Summer day.   9.____
10. He was assisted by his friend, who lives in the next house.   10.____

KEY (CORRECT ANSWERS)

1. B   6. A
2. B   7. C
3. C   8. A
4. D   9. C
5. B   10. D

TEST 6

DIRECTIONS: Each of the sentences in this test may be classified under one of the following four categories:
- A. Faulty because of incorrect grammar or word usage
- B. Faulty because of incorrect punctuation
- C. Faulty because of incorrect capitalization or incorrect spelling
- D. Correct

Examine each sentence carefully to determine under which of the above four options it is best classified. Then, in the space to the right, print the capital letter preceding the option which is the BEST of the four suggested above. (Note that each faulty sentence contains but one type of error. Consider a sentence to be correct if it contains none of the types of errors mentioned, even though there may be other correct ways of expressing the same thought.)

1. The climate of New York is colder than California. 1.____
2. I shall wait for you on the corner. 2.____
3. Did we see the boy who, we think, is the leader. 3.____
4. Being a modest person, John seldom talks about his invention. 4.____
5. The gang is called the smith street bos. 5.____
6. He seen the man break into the store. 6.____
7. We expected to lay still there for quite a while. 7.____
8. He is considered to be the Leader of his organization. 8.____
9. Although I recieved an invitation, I won't go. 9.____
10. The letter must be here some place. 10.____

KEY (CORRECT ANSWERS)

1.	A	6.	A
2.	D	7.	A
3.	B	8.	C
4.	D	9.	C
5.	C	10.	A

TEST 7

DIRECTIONS: Each of the sentences in this test may be classified under one of the following four categories:
  A. Faulty because of incorrect grammar or word usage
  B. Faulty because of incorrect punctuation
  C. Faulty because of incorrect capitalization or incorrect spelling
  D. Correct

Examine each sentence carefully to determine under which of the above four options it is best classified. Then, in the space to the right, print the capital letter preceding the option which is the BEST of the four suggested above. (Note that each faulty sentence contains but one type of error. Consider a sentence to be correct if it contains none of the types of errors mentioned, even though there may be other correct ways of expressing the same thought.)

1. I though it to be he. 1._____
2. We expect to remain here for a long time. 2._____
3. The committee was agreed. 3._____
4. Two-thirds of the building are finished. 4._____
5. The water was froze. 5._____
6. Everyone of the salesmen must supply their own car. 6._____
7. Who is the author of Gone With the Wind? 7._____
8. He marched on and declaring that he would never surrender. 8._____
9. Who shall I say called? 9._____
10. Everyone has left but they. 10._____

KEY (CORRECT ANSWERS)

1.	A	6.	A
2.	D	7.	B
3.	D	8.	A
4.	A	9.	D
5.	A	10.	D

TEST 8

DIRECTIONS: Each of the sentences in this test may be classified under one of the following four categories:
- A. Faulty because of incorrect grammar or word usage
- B. Faulty because of incorrect punctuation
- C. Faulty because of incorrect capitalization or incorrect spelling
- D. Correct

Examine each sentence carefully to determine under which of the above four options it is best classified. Then, in the space to the right, print the capital letter preceding the option which is the BEST of the four suggested above. (Note that each faulty sentence contains but one type of error. Consider a sentence to be correct if it contains none of the types of errors mentioned, even though there may be other correct ways of expressing the same thought.)

1. Who did we give the order to? 1.____
2. Send your order in immediately. 2.____
3. I believe I paid the Bill. 3.____
4. I have not met but one person. 4.____
5. Why aren't Tom, and Fred, going to the dance? 5.____
6. What reason is there for him not going? 6.____
7. The seige of Malta was a tremendous event. 7.____
8. I was there yesterday I assure you 8.____
9. Your ukulele is better than mine. 9.____
10. No one was there only Mary. 10.____

KEY (CORRECT ANSWERS)

1. A   6. A
2. D   7. C
3. C   8. B
4. A   9. C
5. B   10. A

TEST 9

DIRECTIONS: In each of the following groups of sentences, one of the four sentences is faulty in grammar, punctuation, or capitalization. Select the INCORRECT sentence in each case.

1. A. If you had stood at home and done your homework, you would not have failed in arithmetic.
   B. Her affected manner annoyed every member of the audience.
   C. How will the new law affect our income taxes?
   D. The plants were not affected by the long, cold winter, but they succumbed to the drought of summer.

   1.____

2. A. He is one of the most able men who have been in the Senate.
   B. It is he who is to blame for the lamentable mistake.
   C. Haven't you a helpful suggestion to make at this time?
   D. The money was robbed from the blind man's cup.

   2.____

3. A. The amount of children in this school is steadily increasing.
   B. After taking an apple from the table, she went out to play.
   C. He borrowed a dollar from me.
   D. I had hoped my brother would arrive before me.

   3.____

4. A. Whom do you think I hear from every week?
   B. Who do you think is the right man for the job?
   C. Who do you think I found in the room?
   D. He is the man whom we considered a good candidate for the presidency.

   4.____

5. A. Quietly the puppy laid down before the fireplace.
   B. You have made your bed; now lie in it.
   C. I was badly sunburned because I had lain too long in the sun.
   D. I laid the doll on the bed and left the room.

   5.____

KEY (CORRECT ANSWERS)

1. A
2. D
3. A
4. C
5. A

GLOSSARY OF SHIPPING TERMS AND ABBREVIATIONS

A

a.a.x - Against all risks
ADDRESS - A particular street address (not a U.S. Post Office Box Number), which must include the Post Office Zip Code.
a.d. - After date.
AD. VAL. - According to value (Ad Valorem).
AD VALOREM - A freight rate set at a certain percentage of the value of an article is known as an ad valorem rate.
ANY QUANTITY - Rates are applicable regardless of quantity or weight.
A.1 - First class condition.
AQ - Any quantity.
AVDP. - Avoirdupois.

B

B&SG - Browne & Sharpe gauge
bbl. - Barrel.
B.D.I. - Both dates inclusive
B/E - Bill of exchange.
B/L - Bill of lading.
B.O. - Bad order; Buyer's option.
B/P - Bills payable.
bu. - Bushel.
BULK CARRIER - A bulk carrier is a vessel engaged in the carriage of such bulk commodities as petroleum, grain, or ores which are not packaged, bundled, bottled, or otherwise packed.
BWG- Birmingham wire gauge
bx. - Box.

C

C&F - Cost and freight; the same as c.i.f., except that insurance
is arranged by the buyer.
c.c. - Current cost.
c.f. - Cubic foot.
c.i. - Cost and insurance.
c/i-Certificate of insurance.
CIF - Cost, insurance, and freight: a price quotation under which the exporter quotes a price that includes prepayment of freight charges and insurance to an agreed destination
c.i.f.& e. - Cost, insurance, freight & exchange.
C.O.D. - Cash on delivery; Collection on delivery.
C.O.S. - Cash on shipment.
C.R. – Carrier's risk.
c.t.l.o. - Constructive total loss only. cu. ft. - Cubic feet.
cwt. - Hundredweight.

D

D.A. - Documents for acceptance.
D/A - Days after acceptance.
DAT - Dangerous articles tariff.
d/b/a - Doing business as.
D.D. - Demand draft.
D/D - Date draft
d.d.e. - Dispatch discharging only.

DEFERRED REBATE - A deferred rebate is the return of a portion of the freight charges by a carrier or a conference to a shipper in exchange for the shipper giving all or most of his shipments to the carrier or conference over a specified period of time (usually six months). Payment of the rebate is deferred for a further similar period, during which the shipper must continue to give all or most of his shipments to the rebating carrier or conference. The shipper thus earns a further rebate which will not, however, be paid without an additional period of exclusive or almost exclusive patronage with the carrier or conference. In this way, the shipper becomes tied to the rebating carrier or conference. Although the deferred rebate system is illegal in U.S. foreign commerce, it generally is accepted in the ocean trade between foreign countries.

DENSITY - Density means pounds per cubic foot.
 The cubage of loose articles or pieces, or packaged articles of a rectangular, elliptical or square shape on one plane shall be determined by multiplying the greatest straight line dimensions of length, width and depth in inches, including all projections, and dividing the total by 1728 (to obtain cubic feet). The density is the weight of the article divided by the cubic feet thus obtained.

d.l.o. - Dispatch loading only.
dm. - Decimeter.
DM. - Dekameter.
DOT - Department of Transportation.
D.P. - Documents for payment.
d.p. - Direct port.
D/S - Days after sight.
d.w. - Deadweight (tons of 2240 lbs.).
d.w.c. - Deadweight for cargo.

E

E.A.O.N. - Expect as otherwise noted.
E.&.O.F. - Errors and omissions excepted.
E.E. - Errors excepted.
e.g. - For example.
est. - Estimated
est. wt. - Estimated weight.
et.al. - And others

F

f.a.c. - Fast as you can.
FAS - Free along side (vessel): a price quotation under which the exporter quotes a price that includes delivery of the goods to the vessel's side and within reach of its loading tackle. Subsequent risks and expenses are for the account of the buyer.
f.d. - Free discharge.
f.i.o. - Free in and out.
f.i.w. - Free in wagon.
FINISHED - Wooden articles that have passed the state of manufacture "in the white."
 (See IN THE WHITE)
F.M. - Fine measurement.
fms. - Fathoms.
FOB - Free on board (vessel) a price quotation under which the exporter quotes a price that includes delivery of the goods on board the vessel. Subsequent risks and expenses are for the account of the buyer. The term FOB may also be used in conjunction with an inland shipping point in the country of exportation or an inland point in the country of destination. This means that the expenses up to the point specified are for the account of the seller.

FOLDED - An article folded in such a manner as to reduce its bulk 33 1/3% from its normal shipping cubage when not folded.
FOLDED FLAT - An article folded in such a manner as to reduce its bulk 66 2/3% from its normal shipping cubage when not folded.
f.o.r. - Free on rail.
f.r.&c.c. - Free on riot & civil commotion.
ft. - Foot.

G

GAUGE - Where tariffs refer to gauge, they mean the U.S. standard Gauge for determining thickness of sheet or plate steel: Browne & Sharpe Gauge for rods and sheets of aluminum copper, brass and bronze; U. S. Steel Wire Gauge for iron and steel wire.
gm. - Gram.
G.T. - Gross ton.

H

hf. - Half.
hhd. - Hogshead.
ht. - Height.

I

ICC - Interstate Commerce Commission.
IN THE ROUGH - Wooden articles that are not further manufactured than sawn, hewn, planed, bent or turned.
IN THE WHITE - Wooden articles that are further manufactured than "in the rough," but including not more than one coat of priming.
inv. - Invoice

K

KD - Knocked down.
kg. - Kilogram.
KD FLAT - An article taken apart, folded or telescoped to reduce its bulk at least 66 2/3% below its assembled size.
KNOCKED DOWN (KD) - An article taken apart folded or telescoped in such a manner as to reduce its bulk at least 33 1/3% below its assembled bulk.

L

L.&D. - Loss and damage.
L.A. - Letter of authority.
L/C - Letter of credit.
L.C.L. - Less than carload.
l.c.m. - Least common multiple.
ldg. - Loading
LESS THAN TRUCKLOAD (LTL) - Rates applicable when the quantity of freight is less than the volume or truckload minimum weight.
LINER - A liner is a vessel, usually a common carrier, engaged in the carriage of general cargo along a definite route on a fixed schedule.
ltge. - Lighterage.
LTL - Less than truckload.

M

M.A. FORM - Special form of invoice required for shipment to Canada.
MDSE. - Merchandise.
MEASUREMENT TON - The measurement ton (also known as the cargo ton or freight ton) is a space measurement, usually 40 cubic feet or one cubic meter. The cargo is assessed a certain rate for every 40 cubic feet of space it occupies.
min. wt. - Minimum weight.
MW - Minimum weight factor.

N

NESTED - Three or more different sizes of an article are placed within each other so that each article will not project above the next lower article by more than 33 1/3% of its height.
NESTED SOLID - Three or more different sizes of an article are placed within each other so that each article will not project above the next lower article by more than 1/4 inch.
NMFC - National Motor Freight Classification.
N.O.E. - Not otherwise enumerated.
N.O.H.P. - Not otherwise herein provided.
N.O.I. - Not more specifically described.
N.O.I.B.N. - Not otherwise indicated by number; Not otherwise indicated by name.
N.O.S. - Not otherwise specified.
N.S.P.F. - Not specifically provided for.

O

O/A - Open account.
O/N - Order notify.
O.R. - Owners Risk.
O.S.&D. - Over, short and damage.
o.t. – On truck or railway

P

P.A. - Particular average.
P.D. - Per diem.
PLACE - A particular street address or other designation of a factory, store, warehouse, place of business, private residence, construction camp or the like, at a point (See POINT).
POINT - A particular city, town, village or other community or area which is treated as a unit for the application of rates.
PPD. - Prepaid.
PRO NUMBER - A number assigned by the carrier to a single shipment, used in all cases where the shipment must be referred to. Usually assigned at once.
P.W. - Packed weight.

R

REFG. - Refrigerating; Refrigeration.
R.I.T. - Refining in transit.
R.S. or L. - Classes the same or lower.

S

S.C. &S. - Strapped, corded and sealed.
S/D - Sight draft.
S.D.D. - Store door delivery.
sdg. - Siding
SET UP - Articles in their assembled condition.
SHIPMENT - A lot of freight tendered to a carrier by one consignor at one place at one time for delivery to one consignee at one place or one bill of lading.
S.I.T. - Stopping in transit.
SITE - A particular platform or location for loading or unloading at a place (See PLACE).
sld. - Sailed.
S.I. &C. - Shipper's load and count.
S.O. - Ship's option; Shipping order; seller's option.
S.S. - Shipside.
S/S - Steamship.
STDS. - Standards.
str. - Steamer.
S.U. - Set up.
S.U.C.I. - Set up carload.
S.U.I.C.L. - Set up in less than carload.

T

t/d/b/a - Trading and doing business as.
TL - Truckload.
t.l.o. - Total loss only.
TON - Freight rates for liner cargo generally are quoted on the basis of a certain rate per ton, depending on the nature of the commodity. This ton, however, may be a weight ton or a measurement ton.
TRAMP - A tramp ship is a vessel that does not operate along a definite route on a fixed schedule, but calls at any port where cargo is available.
TRUCKLOAD - Truckload rates apply where the tariff shows a truckload minimum weight. Charges will be at the truckload minimum weight unless weight is higher.

U

U.S.S.G. - U.S. standard guage.
u/w - Underwriter.

V

val. - Value.
VES. - Vessel.
viz. - Namely.
VOL. - Volume
VOLUME - Volume rates or classes are those for which a volume minimum weight (Vol. min. wt.) is provided; charges will be assessed at the volume minimum weight shown in the tariff except that actual weight will apply when in excess of the volume minimum weight.

W

W.&I. - Weighing and inspection.
W/B - Waybill.
w.p.a. - With particular average.

www.ingramcontent.com/pod-product-compliance
Lightning Source LLC
Chambersburg PA
CBHW082205300426
44117CB00016B/2674